Two week loan

Please return on or before the last
date stamped below.
Charges are made for late return.

IS 239/0799

INFORMATION SERVICES PO BOX 430, CARDIFF CF10 3XT

The Railway Barons

The Railway Barons

DAVID MOUNTFIELD

First published in 1979 by
Osprey Publishing Limited,
12–14 Long Acre, London WC2E 9LP
A Member Company
of the George Philip Group

British Library Cataloguing in Publication Data

Mountfield, David
The railway barons.
1. Railroads – United States – History
2. Capitalists and financiers – United States
– History
3. Railroads – Great Britain – History
4. Capitalists and financiers – History
I. Title
385'.0973   HE2751

ISBN 0–85045–321–6

Filmset and printed by
BAS Printers Limited, Over Wallop,
Hampshire

CONTENTS

Introduction

Of all the vast changes occurring in the countries of the west during the period of the Industrial Revolution the greatest, and the most vitally necessary, was the construction of railways. In Britain, where the techniques of mass production were first successfully employed, there were signs in the 1820s that the tremendous economic impetus spearheaded by the textile industry was beginning to flag. Railways developed just in time to arrest the downward turn and send the economic production graph shooting upwards again even higher than before. Thanks largely to British railway enterprises, at home and abroad, the momentum continued for half a century – though not without the occasional hiccup – and Britain maintained its position of world dominance in manufacturing until the last quarter of the nineteenth century.

Yet, curiously, railways were less vital for Britain than they were for other countries. Britain had a remarkably good system of bulk transportation by water – sea, river and canal – without which the industrial lead it had achieved in the early nineteenth century would have been impossible. It was to a large extent the absence of such a system that held back industrial development in countries such as Germany or the United States. One reason for the rapid construction of railways in Britain was the need to find some outlet for the capital that had been piling up during the commercial expansion of the previous fifty years, but in the

United States the motives were somewhat different. Capital was not particularly plentiful: many railroad companies encountered severe difficulties in raising it, and much of it came from Europe in any case. On the other hand, railways were vitally necessary to join the growing west with the established east, not only to provide quick and inexpensive transport for manufactured goods moving westward and agricultural produce moving eastward, but also for political reasons.

As every intelligent American was aware, national union had been achieved with difficulty and remained fragile. When at last the break came between North and South, it was repaired only after a cruel civil war, and this war might well have been lost by the Union had not the interests of the west been united with the interests of the North. That alliance of farmers and businessmen would hardly have been achieved without the improved communications provided largely by railways in the previous twenty years. After the Civil War, with the construction of transcontinental routes, the railways became the chief agency for colonizing the far west. The plains states and the Pacific north-west would never have been developed without them. Railways were the pre-eminent industry of the century, the *sine qua non* of other industries. The copper-mining boom in Michigan in the 1840s was the direct result of the opening of a railway link with the east, and John D. Rockefeller would never have made even his first million in oil without the railways. As long as barrels had to be carted over mountains or floated down rivers, expansion was strictly limited; the oil industry, like many others, was the creature of the railway.

Once past the initial conservative resistance which all innovations – and for obscure reasons especially innovations in communications – must overcome, the importance of railways was clearly recognized by contemporaries. The term 'mania' in England, or 'fever' in the United States, perfectly described the hysterically optimistic clamour for shares that marked the periodic railway booms. Not to own any railway shares was an unfortunate handicap, almost a social embarrassment. Cartoonists and satirists derided the railway euphoria amusingly, but their sharpest barbs tended to appear when such booms were already declining and a temporary disillusionment settling in.

In the United States, though the share subscription lists were sometimes less easily filled, railways were identified with the

7

notion of 'manifest destiny'. In a recent article in *The Geographical Journal*, J. Valerie Fifer adumbrated the evolution and political implications of the word 'transcontinental', which was seldom applied to what had hitherto been called, less dramatically, 'the Pacific railroad' until after the Civil War. Never mentioned in accounts of the completion of the Union Pacific-Central Pacific line in 1869, the word was popularized in the guide books of George A. Crofutt, whose *Great Trans-Continental Railroad Guide* sold a million copies between 1870 and 1900. Railways rapidly ascended into the realms of popular romance, achieving the status in national mythology reserved in England for ships and the sea, with the legends of 'John Henry', 'Casey Jones', 'The Wreck of the Old 97' and many others commemorated eternally in folk songs corresponding to the sea shanties that celebrated England's maritime heritage.

Yet the story of the railways is in some respects a seamy saga. On the one hand, a magnificent engineering epic; on the other, a tangled swamp of dubious planning, rogueish financing, opportunism, speculation and fraud. It was the system, the British promoter George Hudson claimed, that brought about the downfall of his railway empire, and to some extent at least he was right. The whole business was so novel, so huge and so complicated that the administrative machinery to organize it simply did not exist and had to be invented, usually by men in a hurry, and often lacking in moral scruples, as they went along.

The fact is that railways have always been a problem, though the nature of the problem has changed with passing time. The railways never quite measured up to the extravagant expectations of the public. The western farmers who clamoured for the construction of railways, expected them to end their difficulties at a stroke. However, they were soon to be heard complaining that the railway was ruining them. The battle cries of the Grangers echoed through political halls, as they brought their power to bear to harness the railways to agrarian interests, and in the angry debates over discriminatory rates, rebates, short haul versus long haul, and all the other inflammatory issues, the industrialists soon joined. Basically the argument was a simple one, and could be summed up in a word – charges. How much might the railways reasonably charge their customers for transporting their persons or their goods? The question was simple, the answer not. The row went on until, finally, government stepped in, and the power of setting charges was effectively removed from the railway companies.

In the early period the problem was different. There was no argument about railway charges when the primary purpose was simply to get railways built. But this desperate eagerness to get a railway regardless of cost and without much thought for the future was the root cause of many difficulties. Railway construction became largely a speculative business. A map of England or the United States showing all the lines projected, as well as those actually built, would have to be drawn on a very large scale to accommodate them, and the final result would look like the web of a prodigiously vigorous and totally insane spider. Many of these schemes were so much paper, and their promoters were never very serious about laying track; but as it was, in many parts of both countries, far more lines were built than were actually needed. In the United States, railway lines were often built not as an effect of new settlements but as a means of creating them—not as the servants of civilization but as its spearhead, advancing into regions scarcely explored, where half the workforce was constantly employed beating off the attacks of Indians. Pioneer farmers who hopefully invested in a railroad company in anticipation, not only of dividends on their stock, but of cheap transportation and rapid development of the region, ended up with their investments, for which they had perhaps mortgaged their land, worth nothing as the railroad went bankrupt. In addition, they were compelled to pay what they regarded as excessive charges foisted upon them by rich business magnates in the east who never travelled on the railroad themselves (though they liberally bestowed free passes on their political cronies).

The suspicion and hostility which railroad companies provoked was often well founded. Some companies were economically larger than the states they existed to serve; their presidents were more influential – and better paid – than state governors. When the state of Minnesota, under the influence of the Granger movement, passed a law regulating railroad rates, the president of the Chicago, Milwaukee and St Paul wrote to the governor loftily informing him that his company would ignore the new law until it had been tested by the courts. Railroad companies often virtually controlled the actions of judges and courts, government officials and even legislatures. Their stock was brazenly manipulated to make fortunes for Wall Street jobbers at the expense of the ordinary stockholders. In the circumstances of the time, railroads were so great and powerful as to be, apparently, beyond any man's control.

This was the age of free enterprise, when 'competition' was the god of the market place. Competition would ensure that a good business thrived and a bad business foundered. Competition would protect the consumer and prevent exploitation, since any company that set its profit margins unreasonably high would be undercut by its competitors. There is much to be said for competition, but the plain fact is, as experience proved, that free competition is no way to run a railroad. Competition can only operate effectively when the competitors start off with equal advantages, or disadvantages. With railways, that condition never obtains unless two lines are built parallel between the same terminals; occasionally that did happen, and the usual result was that both companies went bankrupt. Some people recognized the dangers of basing a railway system on competition at a quite early stage. Even George Hudson in the 1840s was, in a weak moment perhaps, prepared to tolerate a certain amount of government regulation, if it meant that his lines would be protected from interlopers. But the belief that competition is the customer's best safeguard was not easily dispelled. For one thing, there seemed to be no tolerable alternative. Hence the tremendous stock-market battles, the takeovers, and the rate wars which peppered the history of the railway industry. The alternative was, of course, government control, and that was the solution (not, as we know, a perfect one) which eventually was adopted in some degree in all countries. It was, however, anathema in the age of free enterprise, and it is difficult to imagine how the railways could have been built in the nineteenth century except by the methods of private enterprise and the joint-stock company.

This book is about the *business* of the early railways, how railway companies were organized, how the lines were constructed and operated. The engineer and the navvy appear only in the wings: builders, bankers and businessmen hold the centre of the stage. There is no attempt at a comprehensive history – a subject hardly to be contemplated except in several large volumes. Rather, it is hoped that by looking at certain outstanding individuals and episodes, a picture may emerge of the means, methods and motives – some admirable, some despicable – of the kind of men who largely controlled the development of railways in Britain and the United States in the nineteenth century and, by the scale of their business enterprises (not to mention their private fortunes), earned themselves the ambiguous title of the Railway Barons.

1 Railway Mania

The early nineteenth century, thought G. M. Young, was the best time for a young Englishman to be born. He assumed, of course, that he could be born into a prosperous family; as in any other period or place, the prospects of a young man of the poorest class were far from promising, and to be born into the family of, say, a casual agricultural labourer in Regency England was as grim a fate as to be born a medieval serf although, given the necessary talent and character, the chances of improving one's position in life were slightly greater. However, for the son of a land-owning squire or of a prosperous draper (like George Hudson), life was full of invigorating opportunity. During the late eighteenth and early nineteenth centuries, Britain had embarked on the experience known as the Industrial Revolution, when economic progress in certain specific industries reached what Professor Rostow called the 'take-off' point, a sudden breakthrough made possible largely by new industrial techniques, a dramatic change of gear into a new, phenomenal rate of growth. The graph of iron production for the years 1780–1850, for example, zooms upward like an ascending rocket; indeed, figures that astonished Britain's jealous continental neighbours in 1830 looked puny twenty years later. Growth rates like this were a complete novelty at that time and, to contemporaries, Britain's industrial leap forward seemed almost miraculous. For those in a position to take advantage of these economic circumstances, the prospect was intoxicating. There seemed no limit to what might be achieved. It was like drinking a glass of champagne while watching the dawn come up.

The sun at dawn casts long shadows. The commercial Englishman, contemplating the great glow on the horizon from his bay window, saw little of the ground in between. In the darkness lay vast and rumbling new cities where thousands of factory workers lived in hastily erected tenements, without churches, parks, sanitation or (until the 1832 Reform Act) political representation, excluded from every form of social activity except one – work. The advantages of the new industrialism were everywhere apparent; the problems were largely overlooked.

Indeed, they were largely unobserved. William Wilberforce knew nothing of the evils of the slave trade until they were brought to his attention through the devoted researches of Thomas Clarkson. Together, they presented the hideous facts to those who had time to read or listen; but the efforts of the Abolitionists can be regarded, not altogether unfairly, as an example of that tendency in society satirized by Dickens in *Bleak House* in the person of Mrs. Jellyby, who was so involved with her foreign philanthropic interests that she disgracefully neglected her own family. Humane people such as Wilberforce were quite simply ignorant of the lives of the industrial working class (a term that had not yet come into general use). There were, of course, voices raised against the growing evils. Robert Owen showed that it was not necessary to grind the workers into the dust in order to run a profitable business, and social reformers such as Edwin Chadwick, who endeavoured to improve the lot of the railway navvies, among others, raised lonely voices inside and outside Parliament to urge the necessity of change.

However, attempts to enact social improvement by legislation ran against the current idea of the appropriate function of government. It would be inaccurate to state that government was not concerned with social legislation – it had made sporadic, but sometimes sweeping, interventions into that area since the Middle Ages – but compared with the modern notion of the welfare state, its role was extremely limited. Measures of social reform often found their way obstructed by that most sacred of sacred cows, the rights of property (a creature often invoked in the debates on railway legislation). In general, the function of government was believed to be essentially passive; the less it interfered the better, and one result of this negative view of government was that, even when reforming laws were passed, they remained merely benign notions, ineffective because unenforced. Thus the Factory Act of 1819, which limited the number of hours that children could work, omitted the clause suggested by Robert Owen that salaried factory inspectors should be appointed to ensure that the act was obeyed, when it finally emerged as law. During the next six years there were precisely two successful prosecutions under the act, although there is no doubt that it was widely disregarded. Parliament took up problems as they arose, hesitantly, often reluctantly, and dealt with them piecemeal, ignoring the larger context and failing to see the long-term trends of which they were frequently merely symptoms. 'There is a gentleman', said the Duke of Wellington of Sir Robert Peel, 'who never sees the end of a campaign,' and that criticism of the greatest political figure of the first half of the nineteenth century might have been applied to government generally. Government tended to do too little and too late, or to do nothing at all, sometimes because to do nothing seemed the best course, sometimes because government simply did not know what to do. The early history of railways in Britain was largely shaped by the relatively passive role of government.

A general reluctance of governments to act was nowhere more evident than in the realm of politics itself. All but a few diehards agreed that a situation in which a largely de-populated village like Old Sarum returned two repre-sentatives to Parliament while the cities of Manchester, Birmingham and Leeds had not a single MP between them was absurd, and it was equally hard to justify the fact that, while some counties had something approaching household suffrage, the member for Edinburgh, for example, was elected by just thirty-three voters. But attempts at political reform were confronted by the barely suppressed terror of the mob which gripped the property-owning classes. Popular distur-bances in 1830 served merely to inflame these fears, and the country teetered on the edge of a political crisis for two years until passage of the Reform Act suddenly released the tensions. Though commonly called the Great Reform Act, it merely abolished the worst anomalies of the system and distributed the vote a little more generously without effecting any significant change in the personnel or policies of government. Its chief accomplishment was to confound the fears of those who thought that political reform would lead to a reign of terror on the lines of the French Revolution (and therefore to make subsequent reform easier). Power remained in the hands of the land-owning gentry and the great merchants (often one and the same), yet the Reform Act showed power beginning to trickle downwards and outwards, embracing those 'middling sort of persons', as Lord Salisbury called them, who had become comfortable, if not rich, as the economy expanded.

One of the prerequisites of the Industrial Revolution was an adequate supply of capital, which was provided by the fortunes built up on commercial enterprise – not least the slave trade – during the eighteenth century. Capital did not come exclusively from great merchants and bankers; in the railway age especially, large amounts were raised from comparatively small investors. There was a large and growing class of people who were able to live in solid bourgeois comfort without working for a living. The National Debt provides a rough index of British prosperity. By the end of the Napoleonic Wars in 1815, the Debt had risen to the truly colossal sum of £876 million; of this, all but about four per cent was held by British subjects, and of those, according to the official figures of 1829, ninety per cent were receiving annual interest of less than £200. From the resources of such moderate capitalists came no small proportion of the funds of the early railway companies.

Another precondition for the Industrial Revolution, no less vital than capital, was adequate transportation. 'Nothing,' said a railway company director in 1841, 'nothing, next to religion, is of so much importance as a ready communication.' Transport before the railways depended on horse and boat – independently or, as on the canals, in conjunction. In England by about 1830 these pre-industrial methods of transport had achieved a considerable capacity. It is often forgotten in all the excitement over the birth of railways that, during the first thirty years of the nineteenth century, Britain enjoyed the

The British mail-coaches introduced by John Palmer provided the fastest system of public transport on land the world had seen. The famous Quicksilver Devonport Mail *allegedly refused to stop for a passenger whose hat and wig had blown off*

benefits of the most efficient system of land transport that the world had yet seen. It depended largely on two developments, the improvement of roads and the use of coaches drawn by four horses which were changed for a fresh team every ten miles or so along the road. Journey times between the provinces and London were dramatically reduced. In the middle of the eighteenth century it took four days to travel by the rare and uncomfortable public coaches from London to Shrewsbury, a distance of about 150 miles. A new coach introduced in 1764, and probably spending longer hours on the road, cut the time in half. When the fast and prestigious mail coaches were introduced in the 1780s, running through the night and making only brief stops, a Londoner could leave town at eight in the evening and dine the following night (at a slightly later hour) in Shrewsbury. By the 1820s, thanks to reconstruction of the road, the time was reduced to eighteen hours, and the *Wonder*, one of the most famous of stage-coaches, lopped another three hours off the journey soon afterwards. By 1835 the *Wonder* had improved its performance by two hours, but three years later it met its match when the London-Birmingham Railway opened. Though on one memorable day, the *Wonder*, leaving London at the same time as the train, actually succeeded in reaching Birmingham first; the writing was on the wall. A few months later, the famous old stage-coach was reduced to the ignominy of being transported as far as Birmingham on a railway truck, and soon it was withdrawn altogether, since everyone was travelling by train.

No less impressive than the speed of the main-road coach services was their increase in numbers. In the mid-eighteenth century many large towns were unconnected with London by stage-coaches, and in the more remote parts of the country the appearance of a coach caused amazement and bewilderment. 'Come and see the house on wheels,' the fishermen's wives in Falmouth called to each other when the Danish consul appeared in such a vehicle in the 1760s. By 1830, some 300 coaches daily passed through the tollgates at Hyde Park Corner alone – the gates had to be kept permanently open – and the total number of coaches leaving London daily exceeded 1,500. The *Wonder* was only one of more than forty that went to Birmingham.

Road transport in the first half of the nineteenth century affords a good illustration of the dictum that during the Industrial Revolution industries expanded to meet growing demand by the improvement of traditional methods until a point was reached at which a technological breakthrough occurred through pressing need; whereupon the industry was lifted on to an entirely new plane. The expansion and improvement of coach services was remarkable by almost any standards, but coaches and horses could only accomplish so much. By comparison with railways, they were slow, uncomfortable, limited in capacity and, above all, expensive. The coming of the railways killed the long-distance coaches almost at a stroke, though overall there was probably an increase in horse-drawn traffic, much of it performing local journeys to and from the railway station.

Coaches carried only passengers – and the mail. Besides passenger luggage, there was room only for the odd parcel and for other nefarious cargoes, such as a brace of salmon bought from a poacher for profitable resale in London. Overland freight was carried by other means. Packhorses were still to be seen in hilly districts picking their way along bridle paths, but more often goods travelled by carrier's wagon. These unwieldy vehicles, with their wide wheels (prescribed by law, to protect the road surface) and their teams of eight or more plodding horses, made slow progress. When Smollett's hero, Roderick Random, was on his way south to London with his friend Strap, they inquired at an inn if any cheap transport was available and were told that the wagon from Newcastle to London had halted there two nights before. If they walked briskly, they would overtake it the next day or, at most, the day after – as indeed they did. A single packhorse carried two or three hundredweight, while a wagon might carry perhaps as much as two tons on a good road. Their capacity compared very unfavourably with that of a river boat drawn by a single horse which, provided it did not have to contend with a strong current, might draw thirty tons or more.

England has been uniquely fortunate in its natural facilities for transport by water. Wherever you go in England, you can never be more than about seventy miles from the sea, and the country has, in addition, numerous navigable rivers. For the first reason, much long-distance traffic was coastal: Newcastle sent coal to London via the North Sea in the sturdy colliers on which Captain Cook learned his trade; a merchant sending goods from Norwich to the capital shipped them down the

Horse-drawn wagons on wooden rails were a common sight in coal-mining districts as early as 1700; their unflanged wheels allowed them to travel on roads, too

18

Wensum, along the coast, and up the Thames. During the eighteenth century, too, inland water transport – powered by the contemporary substitute for the not-yet-perfected steam engine, the horse – was much improved. This was not a new development, but the rapid growth in trade and the poor state of the roads encouraged far more ambitious schemes of river improvement than any attempted before, especially in the industrial areas of Yorkshire and Lancashire. Rivers, however, seldom provided the perfect solution to transport difficulties. Apart from the difficulties encountered with landowners and other vested interests, river traffic could not reach many of the new industrial regions which were 400 or 500 feet above sea level. Raw materials and manufactured products then had to be painfully hauled by wagon to the most convenient river port. Rivers, even the comparatively placid English rivers, are, moreover, unpredictable. The Severn, for instance, the main waterway of the West Country, is particularly susceptible to sudden rises and falls, and was sometimes only navigable for two or three months in the year. Accelerating economic growth after about 1750, especially in the textile industry, and the pressing need for fuel which, if not satisfied, would have strangled the Industrial Revolution at birth, made better and cheaper transport essential.

Canals seemed to promise a solution. Artificial waterways of some size had been built in a few places since the sixteenth century, but the first ambitious canal scheme was constucted in the 1750s in the neighbourhood of Liverpool. A hundred years earlier, the Lancashire port had been hardly more than a village, but during the eighteenth century it thrived mightily on the triangular trade between West Africa and the West Indies, based chiefly on slaves and sugar. By 1750, it had far outstripped Bristol to become the biggest port in England after London. But Liverpool needed coal and the canals built in the 1750s gave it valuable access to some of the Lancashire coalfields.

At about the same time, there appeared upon the scene the Duke of Bridgewater, together with his brilliant self-educated engineer James Brindley. The Duke planned to link the coalfields on his estate at Worsley Park with the eager markets of Liverpool and Manchester. Brindley managed the job, and, with the opening of the first stretch of the Bridgewater

19

Canal in 1761, the canal-building era really began. By flinging an aqueduct over the River Irwell and successfully crossing a stretch of near-swamp, Brindley demonstrated that the canal was a more flexible means of transport than almost anyone had dreamed. The price of coal in Manchester immediately fell by half.

Canal-building proceeded thereafter at a rapid pace. The Staffordshire and Worcester Canal linked the Mersey with the Severn in 1772; the remarkable Trent and Mersey Canal (one of the few to compete successfully with the railways) joined Hull to Liverpool, by a somewhat indirect route, in 1777; the Thames and Severn Canal provided through water-transport between Bristol and London in 1789. By 1830, over 4,000 miles of navigable waterways – canals and rivers – were in use, with 20,000 or more barges working on them, transporting annually about thirty million tons of freight, of which coal represented the largest single commodity.

The canals, like the first railways, were built exclusively for freight transport. In most places, passenger traffic was of no more significance than freight carried by road, but there were some exceptions, especially in Scotland. A canal running through Paisley to Glasgow was equipped with light boats, which were designed for passengers and drawn by pairs of trotting horses, changed like coach horses at frequent intervals. In winter, ice boats were put out to clear a passage for them. They were more comfortable and cheaper than travel by coach, and apparently not much slower (they were said to proceed at nine miles an hour). But this method of travel, obviously limited in potential, had other drawbacks – one being the stench rising from the increasingly black and filthy water of the canal. And, as with the stage-coaches, passenger-traffic on canals did not survive the coming of the railways.

The period of canal building was, in many ways, something of a trial run for the railway age, and many characteristics of financing and engineering usually associated with the later period can, in fact, be traced back to the canals. As with the early railway companies, the lead in forming a canal company was usually taken by prominent local citizens – businessmen anxious to secure cheaper materials or easier access to markets. The far-sighted Duke of Bridgewater was merely the first and most famous of them. As a rule, most of the capital was raised locally, although in the early 1790s, when there was a 'canal mania' comparable with the later 'railway manias', investment in canals became more popular and therefore more widespread. Shares were usually issued for large amounts – £50, £100 or £200 – which meant that shareholders were people of some wealth.

More often than not, the cost of construction exceeded the original estimates, frequently by embarrassing proportions (the Rochdale Canal cost more than double). This was another feature shared by early railway companies. One method adopted to raise the extra capital was by means of preference shares, so-called because the shareholder is guaranteed payment of dividends before other commitments are fulfilled (usually at a fixed rate, so that, if the company is more profitable than expected, the preference shareholder gains his extra security at the expense of participation in the extra profits). This device, usually associated with the railway age, was thus perfectly familiar before the railways were built.

The government sometimes contributed to the cost of building canals which had some special strategic significance, such as Telford's Caledonian Canal (something of a white elephant as things turned out), but otherwise played no part in the business. It has been said that this *laissez-faire* attitude had some advantages; it meant, for instance, that canals tended to be built where local interests required them, rather than according to some scheme, like General Wade's highways in Scotland (or possibly the modern motorway system), in which local interests counted for nothing. On the other hand, the total absence of central planning produced a vast number of infuriating anomalies, and since the canals, unlike the railways, never underwent subsequent amalgamation and rationalization on any scale, they continued as long as the canals remained in use. Professor Bagwell cites the example of a barge proceeding from London to Liverpool shortly before the First World War: there were three possible routes, but on each of them the barge had to pay tolls to at least nine different canal companies. Between Leeds and Liverpool in the early nineteenth century, the locks on the various canals involved could accommodate boats of a maximum length of, successively, seventy-six feet, sixty-six feet, fifty-three feet,

Canals seemed to provide an adequate means of freight transport, but the railways checked their development. This primitive pound lock, with tree trunks for levers, was in use in the 1870s

seventy-three feet, and fifty-three feet. A French visitor, while expressing keen admiration for the canal system as a whole, pondered on the lack of harmony in the varying sizes of locks, canals, tunnels and so on, and concluded that 'the very nature of English institutions is in opposition to such a harmony'.

The canals removed a certain amount of traffic from the rivers, to the consternation of towns and villages that lost trade as a result, but considerably more from the roads. Water transport was everywhere much cheaper. To move goods from Basingstoke to London in 1792 cost £2 a ton by road but less than twelve shillings by the Basingstoke Canal, and that substantial saving was not untypical. The regions that benefited most were the industrial regions of the Midlands, comparatively far from the sea. It was largely the canals that were responsible for the growth of industry in the Black Country, that allowed the Staffordshire potteries to obtain china clay cheaply from Cornwall, and permitted the rapid growth of cities such as Birmingham. The canals not only carried manufactures to market and brought back raw

22

materials or fuel, they also transported most of the food from the farming regions or the ports to the new industrial cities. They had besides many incidental, less obvious advantages. One inhabitant of a canal-side village, for example, rejoiced that since coal had become accessible and cheap, his nostrils were no longer assailed by the stench of burning cow-dung from cottage hearths.

Canals very largely created the profession of civil engineer. Early railway construction was to have its problems, but they would have been vastly greater if engineers had not had the experience of constructing locks, embankments, aqueducts, tunnels, even hydraulic lifts, for the canals. Brindley had astonished the world with his aqueduct crossing the Irwell at the dizzy height of twenty-eight feet. Forty years later, Thomas Telford (the first president of the Institution of Civil Engineers) carried the Ellesmere Canal over the River Dee at a height of 127 feet – on an iron aqueduct. Even the railways could hardly offer more remarkable examples of technological progress. Long before the railways made them famous, British engineers were in demand abroad. Telford himself was hired to build the Gothenburg Canal in Sweden on the strength of his work on the Caledonian Canal.

Some canals were extremely profitable. Unlike roads, they were not deserted when the railways came; there were even a few instances of increased traffic *after* the rival rails had been laid, though such bonuses were usually short-lived and resulted from relaxation of restrictions once the government's fear of a possible transport monopoly had been dissolved by the advent of the railways. The best time for the canal companies was around 1830, just before the railways, when several of them were paying dividends of over twenty-five per cent at a time when five per cent was considered to be a good rate of interest. These were exceptional cases, though a good many other canal companies were paying solid if less sensational returns. However, they would have done better to have ploughed back more of their profits into improvements which would have offered a stronger challenge to railways. Of other companies, this criticism could not be made as they never produced any profits. In general, and as one might expect, canals tended to be most successful on main through routes and in the heavily industrialized regions. Elsewhere, in much of the south of England for example, some companies never managed to pay the interest on loans out of their income, never mind dividends to shareholders.

In the contest of road versus rail, the railways won hands down at almost every point – a verdict which was not to be reversed until the twentieth century. Between rail and water transport, the contest was far less unequal. In capacity, reliability and cost, the canals ran the railways close. They had, indeed, certain advantages. A canal system is less labour-intensive than a railway system, and barges cost less to maintain than railway wagons. On the other hand, canals are less flexible. It is much easier to lay rails than dig a canal, and viaducts are cheaper than aqueducts. Telford's Pont Cysyllt had demonstrated what miracles could be accomplished in bridging topographical gaps for canals, but its cost was enormous and it remained an exception: for the most part, canals did not attempt to cross deep valleys.

A crucial factor was speed. The average canal boat proceeded at a horse's steady plod, two or three miles an hour only. Faster boats could have been and, in some cases, were built, while steam engines were advocated by some to replace the horses. But the simple fact was that the canals themselves were not constructed for greater speeds. In British conditions, there was no potential for the paddle steamer which had such a dramatic effect on transportation in the United States, as the smaller canals could not cope with anything faster than the horse-drawn barge. However, for bulky, low-price cargoes, speed was not essential, and that was the chief reason why canals survived throughout the nineteenth century, carrying over ten per cent of freight tonnage as late as 1898. Slowness, of course, is hardly a virtue, but where they were given a fighting chance, canals were able to carry certain cargoes at a lower rate than the railways. So far as passenger traffic was concerned, the canals never offered a serious challenge to the stage-coach, except on a handful of short routes, and no one could pretend that they competed with railways. That would hardly have mattered, as canals were for practical purposes exclusively designed for freight, but in the early period of competition between canal and railway, the railway companies had the advantage of being able to drive their rivals to the wall by undercutting their freight charges and recouping the resulting loss in increased passenger fares.

Wordy but fierce battles were fought by the supporters of canals (and coaches) against the railways, on the whole without avail; the railway companies sometimes employed skilled propagandists, and the arguments on both sides were not always notable for judicious reasoning. Nowadays, ironically, the case for canals is seen to be a better one than most neutral contemporaries realized, and the gradual decline into which the canals fell is regarded as a matter for regret on plain economic grounds. The relative failure of the canals is largely ascribed to government action – or lack of it – especially in permitting so many canals to pass into railway ownership (some forty per cent of navigable waterways were railway-owned in 1870). This was a notable feature of the 'railway mania' of the 1840s, when Parliament's fear of a transport monopoly proved to be weaker than its reluctance to interfere with the workings of free enterprise.

The introduction of public railways was based on two revolutionary innovations – railway lines and the steam engine. They now appear as an inseparable combination, but they were not seen as such in the early nineteenth century. The rule of the steam engine in transport was forecast long before the opening of the Stockton and Darlington Railway in 1825. As early as 1769 the French engineer, N. J. Cugnot, had produced a mobile steam engine. This was considered by the French army as an artillery carriage, but in view of its limitations, not very seriously, as its top speed was less than three miles an hour and it tended to overturn even then. Moreover, it could keep up steam for only fifteen minutes. In England, William Murdoch, an able mechanic who had worked at the celebrated Birmingham firm of Boulton and Watt, made a small three-wheeled engine that towed a little waggon around his home in 1784. However, Boulton and Watt were not interested; Watt, who was always rather nervous of high-pressure steam engines (justifiably so, since they were then made of brittle cast iron), had a powerful aversion to steam-driven vehicles and, when he was letting his house, he wrote a clause into the lease to forbid any such horrors appearing on his property.

The first steam locomotive that transported passengers seems to have been built by the brilliant Cornish inventor,

Richard Trevithick, temperamentally the opposite of the cautious Watt. But it suffered continual mechanical break-downs and Trevithick concluded that if steam locomotives had a future, it lay on rails, not roads. History was to prove him right, but a great many people thought differently, and if we abolish the advantage of hindsight it is not difficult to see why. One great advantage of steam carriages pointed out by the Birmingham *Advertiser* as late as 1833 (the year the London and Birmingham Railway was authorized) was that they would not require the construction of a totally new network of routes with consequent destruction of property, enormous costs in construction and maintenance of rails, loss of valuable land, and inconvenience to the public, who would still have to use roads to get to the railway. A good case could be made for the economy of steam carriages. In theory at least they could be run more cheaply than either a stage-coach or a railway engine. They had shown themselves capable of maintaining a steady twelve miles an hour and one of them, the *Automaton* of Walter Hancock, was said to have kept up a brisk twenty-five miles an hour while taking some supporters to a cricket match.

Nevertheless, the steam carriage was puffing up a road that led nowhere. Its supporters blamed the hostility of the landowners and the turnpike trusts, who slapped on punitive tolls with the excuse that steam carriages destroyed the road surface, but the real trouble lay in the failure of the steam carriage to overcome technical problems, in particular the incessant breakdowns that resulted from a combination of the comparative mechanical fragility of the early engines and the constant jolting inflicted on their mechanism by the roads, surfaced as they were with gravel for the benefit of horses' hooves and the iron-shod wheels of carriages and carts.

The feasibility of a railway track at first had nothing to do with steam engines, and it is possible that a British national railway network would have been built if locomotives had never been invented. Coal trucks had run on wooden railways since the early seventeenth century (even earlier than this in Germany), when Huntingdon Beaumont, 'a gentleman of great ingenuity and parts', is said to have pioneered them in Nottinghamshire. By the eighteenth century they were common in the coalfields. But wooden railways were not very long-lasting; they broke or soon wore out. The first attempt to

strengthen them involved laying an iron plate along the top, much as wagon wheels were reinforced; then, about 1770, cast-iron plate rails were introduced. These had a rim on the edge to hold the wagons on the rails, a method which had the advantage of allowing the wagons to move over the ground as well as on rails. A different system prevailed in the Newcastle area where the flanged wagon wheel, running on flat rails, was preferred. By 1810, when George Stephenson went to work on the steam pumps at Killingworth, there were several railways over ten miles long on Tyneside, as well as others in a number of other industrial areas such as South Wales. Trevithick tested his locomotive on the Cardiff and Merthyr line in 1804, and a later model, named *Catch-Me-Who-Can*, was afterwards to be seen in London on the very appropriate site of Euston Square. A fee was charged to watch the little engine puffing around its circular railway behind a high wooden fence, but it was regarded as little more than a fairground curiosity. Indeed Trevithick, a brilliant butterfly, soon turned his attention elsewhere, leaving the field to George Stephenson.

In 1825, there were 225 miles of railway on Tyneside (where there were virtually no canals), with points and crossings, a substantial bridge and at least one tunnel. Between Brecon and Hay there was a line twenty-four miles long, including a short tunnel, which might be regarded as an early public railway – it carried passengers and a variety of goods, and was not, like most other railways of the time, dependent for economic survival solely on transporting coal or iron ore – except for the fact that the motive power was provided by horses. Steam power, however, was being advocated by a growing number of enthusiasts.

With Hancock, Goldsworthy Gurney was the most famous of the designers of steam road carriages. This version, drawing a barouche containing the Duke of Wellington among others, ran briefly on the London-Bath road in 1831

Trevithick's locomotive performing in Euston Square in 1809; after Rowlandson

The construction of rail *ways* was pretty well understood; the rails themselves were still a problem. The main disadvantage of cast-iron rails is their brittleness, and they thus share some of the drawbacks of wooden rails. The production of satisfactory wrought-iron rails was difficult and although by 1825, when the Stockton and Darlington Railway opened, the technical problems had been largely overcome, many people still advocated the cast-iron plate rail. It was, indeed, adequate for the average colliery traffic, but the victory of the locomotive, at this time far from assured, was to make the sturdier wrought-iron rails essential.

The Stockton and Darlington is usually regarded as the first public railway, but it was really, as Michael Robbins put it, the curtain-raiser rather than the first act. Although it did use locomotives, it also had stationary steam engines to haul carriages up two inclines, and carried horse-drawn traffic as well. In fact, passengers were still travelling in carriages drawn by horses on the Stockton and Darlington as late as 1856. Incidentally, the quantity of passengers proved an unexpected bonus, as railways were still thought of as primarily conveyors of freight; the Stockton and Darlington was designed to carry coal from the Durham collieries to the coast.

In 1828, when much of the Liverpool and Manchester railway had already been built, the engineer, George Stephenson, had still not convinced the promoters that steam traction was the best alternative. He had built his first locomotive on Tyneside in 1814 and more than twenty, including those supplied to the Stockton and Darlington, since then, but the battle for the locomotive was far from won. The parliamentary bill for the Newcastle-Carlisle Railway in 1829 contained a clause actually forbidding the employment of a locomotive engine, and although that provision was probably forced on the company by landowners anxious to preserve their peace and quiet, the promoters clearly did not regard locomotives as essential.

The Stockton and Darlington Railway, opened in 1825, employed locomotives for a short stretch only, stationary steam engines being employed on inclines

J. R. Brown

George Stephenson, from the portrait by H. W. Vickersgill. More than anyone, he was responsible for the rapid growth of railways, but the 'Railway Mania' provoked his stern disapproval

The Liverpool businessmen who were behind the Liverpool and Manchester called in two experts from London for an outside opinion. They reported in favour of stationary engines with cables, although they did admit that locomotives seemed to have better potential. George Stephenson and his supporters, however, made mincemeat of their report. From our later viewpoint, the battle seems one-sided. Apart from the inconvenience of cable-hauled wagons (Stephenson made some sarcastic comments about the spider's web likely to result at points and crossings), they were more expensive. It would have been necessary to site fifty-four stationary engines along the line between Liverpool and Manchester, and although the number of locomotives estimated as necessary to deal with the anticipated volume of traffic was not much smaller, the cost was far less – £28,000 as against £81,000 for stationary engines. Discussions were long and heated – inevitably so as the company had no less than thirty directors – but the scales tilted steadily in favour of the locomotive. In April 1829 the board offered a prize of £500 for the best locomotive to emerge from a trial held on a completed section of line at Rainhill. Various conditions regarding weight of engine, load and speed had to be met, and another stipulation was that the locomotives should produce no smoke. Thus the common reaction to prints of early railway passengers in open carriages – that they must have suffered shockingly from smut, sparks and smoke – is misplaced. The early locomotives burned coke, not coal.

The Rainhill test attracted a great deal of public interest and a large number of hopeful entrants. When the day arrived, however, most had scratched, and there were only three locomotives left in the field. Of the three engineers involved, Stephenson was far the most experienced. His engine was the *Rocket* (actually the second locomotive of that name he had built) and it was ahead of its rivals in several respects, notably in the use of a multitubular boiler, the prototype for all subsequent locomotive steam boilers though very different in construction. In front of a large crowd, the *Rocket*, easily maintaining the required ten miles an hour, ran away with the prize.

Before a railway could be built, two things were necessary; the required capital, or an assurance of it, and an enabling Act of Parliament. In other countries, railways were often

THE LOCOMOTIVE STEAM ENGINES
Which competed for the Prize of £500 offered by the Directors of the Liverpool and Manchester Railway Comp.ᵞ_ drawn to a Scale ¼ inch to a foot.

The **ROCKET** *of M.ʳ Rob.ᵗ Stephenson of Newcastle.*
Which drawing a load equivalent to three times its weight travelled at the rate of 12½ miles an hour, & with a carriage & passengers at the rate of 24 miles. Cost per mile for fuel about three-halfpence.

supported by government for some reason of national policy, but in Britain they were purely business propositions, and it was necessary to show convincingly that their earnings would be large enough to give a profitable return on the subscribed capital. From a company's point of view, the enabling act was necessary in order to give a firm basis for negotiation with the owners of the land through which the railway would pass; the act normally confirmed right of purchase, although that did not prevent some land-owners from virtually holding a railway company up to ransom (Lord Petre of Ingatestone Hall extracted £120,000 from the Eastern Counties Railway for land worth £5,000). The process of securing the act was nearly always lengthy and expensive, with much intensive lobbying by supporters and opponents of the proposed railway and ample opportunity for obstruction; practical men like Thomas Brassey used to gnash their teeth over these goings-on.

The famous Rocket *of George and Robert Stephenson which established the superiority of the steam locomotive by its performance in the Rainhill trials in 1829*

31

The first bill for the Stockton and Darlington was feverishly debated by a House of Commons Committee for thirty-seven days – and then thrown out. The eventual act ran to sixty-one pages of fairly small print.

The early idea of what a railway should be, as set out in the Stockton and Darlington act, may well seem strange to a later generation. The act authorized incorporation of the railway company, the building of the railway, and the carriage of goods, but it did not explicitly provide for conveyance of passengers; it also assumed that while the company would run the railway, the actual carriage of goods would be performed by others, in a manner analogous to canals or roads. Thus the horse-drawn coaches that carried passengers on the railway belonged to several independent operators, paying tolls to the railway company and operating under licence. There were still privately owned wagons in service on Britain's railways at the time of nationalization in 1947, though it was soon found that haulage was best undertaken by the railway company. Although the act laid down maximum tolls which could be charged to the independent operators, the limits were so high that they were meaningless; nor were the maximum fees to be charged when the railway company was the carrier specified. Another notable omission was the absence of any provision for proper accounting, so for all practical purposes, the company was not accountable to the public or its shareholders. As a result, the railway accounts that were published in the early years were shrouded in a good deal of mystery, though this was perhaps more the result of ignorance or inexperience than a deliberate attempt to mislead. However, until regular skilled auditing became the rule, there was opportunity for fraud on a large scale. To this day it is very difficult, in view of the curious system of accounting employed, to answer even such straightforward questions as whether a certain company was profitable or not, since it is not always certain that dividends were paid, as they legally should have been, out of actual profits.

It is usually said that most railway capital was raised locally. The Stockton and Darlington was called the 'Quakers' Line' because of the large part played by Quaker bankers in Darlington, notably the Pease family. However, although most of its share capital was raised locally, substantial loans were raised elsewhere, chiefly in London. Despite the great influence of Liverpool businessmen, the Liverpool and Manchester Railway secured roughly half its promises of capital from outside Lancashire. The usual method of raising capital in the early days was to organize local public meetings at which investors would buy scrip – exchangeable for future shares – in the proposed company, paying a small deposit. The rest came from the bankers, and the amount that could be raised from them depended on the persuasiveness of the directors, who were, of course, sometimes bankers themselves. Since most companies were floated during booms, there was usually no shortage of subscriptions. On the other hand, in the economic slumps that followed the booms it was the pressure of the railway companies on the capital market that was blamed. This charge, however, was largely unfair on the railway companies. It was really a general economic boom that encouraged railway promotion rather than vice-versa, and the ensuing slump, which was anyway due to wider causes, was to some extent ameliorated by the economic activity generated by the successful railway promotions: to generalize, promotion took place in a boom, construction often in a slump. After about 1850 the situation changed; the main sources of railway capital became increasingly the big, established railway companies themselves and the great contractors, like Brassey and Peto, who were responsible for railway construction.

The lurching progress of railway promotion was the result of changing economic conditions; since investment came largely through the issue of capital stock, it obviously depended on the state of the capital market, itself influenced by a number of different circumstances. A complicating factor was the long delay that inevitably intervened between the first airing of the proposal and the opening of the railway, and especially the time taken securing the necessary Act of Parliament. Once the proposal for a railway had been made, it would take perhaps a year to survey the route and to secure promises of investment. Obtaining the act took at least another year and if, as frequently happened, the first bill was rejected, the promoters were obliged to wait another year before resubmitting it. Hold-ups could occur in any number of ways – difficulty in obtaining sufficient financial support, opposition from land-owners or from rivals such as canal companies, and so on. The bill for the London and Birmingham Railway, for instance, came before the House of Commons in 1832. After a great battle, the combined challenge of land-owners, canal companies and stage-coach operators was defeated, but when the bill went to the House of Lords it was thrown out. The company then made a number of compromises with their various opponents and a new bill was submitted which was passed in 1833. Construction then began, and the railway finally opened in 1838.

There is a school of thought which sees the land-owning aristocracy as the chief opponent of the railways – reaction and privilege confronting social progress. Undoubtedly, in the early years especially, there was some strong opposition from that quarter but its extent can be easily exaggerated. Had the land-owning class stood solidly against railways, none would have been built. In reality, there were probably more land-owners in favour than against. Apart from other considerations, they frequently stood to benefit, not so much by exploiting the railway companies anxious to buy their land as by easier and cheaper communication with their estates.

In spite of the slight air of mystery over their accounts, the Stockton and Darlington and the Liverpool and Manchester proved profitable. There was even some reason to think that the latter was more profitable than it appeared (its Act of Parliament limited its dividend to ten per cent, and the company was accused, perhaps unjustly, of issuing extra dividends disguised as shares), and this profitability led to a boom in the mid-1830s which is usually termed the first 'railway mania' (others regard the rush of promotions following the Stockton-Darlington in the mid-1820s as the first mania). As the deposit required from shareholders was only five per cent (the remainder to be called upon as construction proceeded), it was possible to buy a substantial share in a railway company for a comparatively small sum. This encouraged speculation, for some companies, not subject to the limitations placed on the Liverpool and Manchester, anticipated dividends of twenty per cent or more. During this period of confidence, it was possible to secure financial backing for almost any scheme that could nominally be termed a railway. 'The wildest schemes were calmly entertained,' wrote J. A. Francis. 'One projector proposed sails to propel his engine ... Another offered to propel his locomotives with rockets ... A third invented a wooden line, to be raised many feet from the ground to allow a free and uninterrupted intercourse beneath.' The surprising thing is that of all the companies that got as far as securing their enabling act (thirty-nine in 1836–37), very few could be regarded as complete failures.

The first 'mania' faded in 1837, largely due to a general recession but also partly to some tightening-up by Parliament which resulted from the disturbing rush of new companies (for example, it was agreed that at least ten per cent of the capital had to be paid up before an act of incorporation could be passed), and from some shocks, such as the announcement by the London and Birmingham Railway, then under construction, that its capital requirements had doubled. The Eastern Counties Railway, authorized in 1836, was the largest company to suffer from the rapid dissipation of railway euphoria. It was unable to sell all its authorized shares, and when it called on a fairly modest £16 on £25 shares, the total receipts fell way short of the sum this should have brought in. It proved impossible to raise substantial loans, and construction petered out. By 1843, less than half the projected track mileage had been built, and it was decided to cancel the remainder.

This first mania convinced most people that there ought to be more public regulation of railways. The acts of incorporation of each company not only allowed them a fairly free rein, but carried no measures of enforcement, and critics of the companies believed, rightly or wrongly, that many conditions laid down in such acts were widely evaded. In 1840, a Railway Department was created in the Board of Trade. It had a staff of just three men, and in practice its only important function was to inspect the railways in the interests of public safety. Even the Duke of Wellington, complaining, rather late in the day, that railways were killing coaches, said he thought the scope of the act was too restricted.

The early 1840s were a time of economic depression. Some disillusion with railways was widely expressed: almost without exception they had proved more expensive to build than estimated and had failed to return the profits that had originally been forecast. Many people believed that the railway network as it existed was more or less complete, a misapprehension that, before the end of the decade, seemed staggering. But although railway dividends were low, in most cases they were higher than interest on government stocks (the Eastern Counties Railway being one obvious exception), which was under two and a half per cent in 1842–43. At that time railway shares were beginning to move up again, and railways began to look an increasingly attractive investment. Moreover, the ten per cent of capital required to be deposited before a railway company could be authorized was reduced by W. E. Gladstone, then President of the Board of Trade, to five per cent. By the end of 1844, a real railway mania, far greater than that of 1836, was under way.

Paradoxically, it was encouraged by Gladstone's act of 1844 which, though much watered down in its final form, was intended to ensure that railways were controlled in the public interest. It gave the government the right to revise a company's charges after twenty-one years if it was making a consistent annual profit of ten per cent or more, and also to buy the railway after an equivalent period on payment of compensation to be based on profits over a fixed period, assuming, again, that average profits were at least ten per cent annually. This obtrusive figure of ten per cent inadvertently conveyed the impression that the government confidently expected the railway companies to achieve that high annual rate of profit, and so encouraged the railway mania. A Klondike atmosphere rapidly developed.

The extent of the mania is most easily indicated by statistics of total railway mileage authorized by parliamentary acts. In 1843 this figure was less than 100 miles; in 1844 it rose to over 800; in the following year it was nearly 3,000; and in 1846 over 4,500. The number of railway promotions canvassed, many of which never got as far as Parliament, was naturally far greater. A list compiled at the end of 1845 indentified over 1,000 railway projects of various kinds with total capital of over £700 million. The significance of such a figure is difficult to grasp today, since inflation has so far reduced the value of money, but some idea of its scale becomes apparent if we recall that it represented over ten times the total value of annual exports from the United Kingdom in 1847. Of course, the majority of these projects never materialized, and the list undoubtedly included many that were doubtful in the extreme.

Some schemes were promoted solely to block competition or to prevent a rival company encroaching on the business of one already established on the scene. In fact, most of the new lines were promoted by existing companies, and there was a strong movement in favour of monopoly. The banker George Carr Glyn, the chairman of the London and Birmingham, told a House of Commons Committee that new lines ought to be constructed by established railway companies, and insisted that competition was undesirable since it encouraged rate-cutting which led to deterioration of standards. Parliament was not unsympathetic to this view. Another feature of the mania of the

37

1840s was the merger of companies – an area in which George Hudson was particularly active.

This was the era of the 'traffic-takers', who were employed to estimate the likely traffic in an area where a railway was projected. They often took an absurdly rosy view of the prospects as satirically related by one of the big railway 'barons', Edward Watkin, speaking at the National Conference of Railway Shareholders in 1868: '... there were gentlemen who rode in their carriages and kept fine establishments who were called "traffic takers". . . . One of these gentlemen in 1844 ... was sent to take the traffic on a railway called the Manchester and Southampton. It did not go to Manchester and it did not go to Southampton; but it was certainly an intermediate link between these places. This gentleman went to a place in Wilts where there was a fair, and there took the number of sheep on the fair day, and assuming that there would be the same number all the days of the year, he doubled or trebled the amount for what he called "development" [laughter] and the result was that he calculated that by sheep alone the Manchester and Southampton line would pay fifteen per cent.'[1]

The speculative climate was feverish, and cartoonists had a field day depicting its sillier aspects. One showed the Queen reproaching a despondent Prince Albert because he had failed to acquire any railway shares. No one wanted to be left out of the railway bonanza, and the shares of the established companies rocketed. Dividends soared also, though this was sometimes achieved by dubious accounting methods. Naturally, railways were constantly discussed in Parliament. The Board of Trade was hardly able to cope with the avalanche of promotions on which it was supposed to pass judgement, and its officials, subject to fierce attack by the railway interest in Parliament, were not always convincingly supported by the Prime Minister, Peel, who was in general favourably inclined to the railway companies. Parliament, according to Sir John Clapham, was 'dazed with the roar of the railways and the chink of their promoters' pence'. Astonishing scenes took place on November 30, the last day of the year on which plans for new railways could be deposited at the offices of the Board of Trade. The roads into London were blocked and in Whitehall it was impossible to move for the crush of eager promoters.

[1] *See Bibliography p. 219 for sources of keyed quotations.*

*The 'Railway Mania'
was a boon to
cartoonists. The young
Queen Victoria is
pictured asking a
dejected Prince Albert if
he has any railway
shares*

The mania, inevitably, was short-lived. Floated on euphoric clouds, most of the projects would never have got off the ground in any case, and in 1847 they were cut off by a precipitate slump. The mania, proclaimed Lord Morley in his *Life of Gladstone* 'was even more widely disastrous than any ... investment had been since the days of the South Sea Bubble'. More recently economic historians have shown that, despite the fearful pressure on the capital market that the mania exerted, there were other causes for the slump. The repeal of the Corn Laws in 1846 was followed by huge imports of food (and by falling domestic prices, with disastrous effects

39

on those involved in the corn trade). At about the same time, a shortage in the supply of American cotton sent prices up sharply. These and other factors were responsible for a fierce rise in the import bill which caused a frightening drain of reserves; for a moment it seemed likely that the Bank of England would have to clamp down totally on loans. The financial panic was brief, but it effectively ended the railway mania. Total authorized mileage slipped from its peak of over 4,500 miles in 1846 to 1,295 in 1847. The following year it fell below 300, and in 1849 it was just seventeen. Share prices fell by half between 1846 and 1849, and so did dividends.

Shock and dismay were evident all around, but the most notable feature of the post-mania years was that, on the whole, construction of railways authorized during the peak years was carried on. Some desperate devices were sometimes necessary to raise money, such as the payment of creditors in railway stock, and the changed climate was evident in the tone of pride with which one company announced that it had fewer works in progress than any other company of comparable size. Another important effect of the slump was that shareholders asserted themselves in meetings to insist that capital expenditure was kept within bounds and that accounts were properly audited by independent experts. Various scandals came to light. But the railways were not dead, far from it. In spite of the much lower dividends, railway investment was still a relatively attractive proposition. Towns the railways had passed by clamoured for new lines as eagerly as they had in the days of the boom. There was a minor boom in railway promotion in the early 1850s and another in the 1860s, followed by an even more disastrous slump. Nevertheless, it was in the optimistic years between 1844 and 1847 that the real revolution in transport and communications took place and the modern railway network of Great Britain was created.

2 Collapse of a Kingdom: The Rise and Fall of George Hudson

George Hudson was the personification of the *nouveau riche*. Fashionable people privately laughed at him; in an approximation of his rough Yorkshire accent his conversational gaffes, alleged or real, were repeated in clubs and drawing-rooms by the same people who sought his help and advice with their investments and profited from his promotional activities. Superficially, indeed, he was an obvious butt. Short and fat, he had a cannon-ball of a head set square upon his bulky shoulders – 'the formality of a neck having been dispensed with', as someone observed. He walked with apparent difficulty, like a mechanical doll, his arms swinging vigorously in the effort to maintain the momentum of his large trunk above his short legs; yet he covered the ground with impressive speed. He had many of the characteristics of the super-salesman or the career politician – volcanic energy, a way of disregarding obstacles, a capacity for directing several different operations (or even conducting two con-versations) simultaneously, and a fondness for lavish, highly publicized entertainments. Though uncouth, tactless and often rude, he had a streak of Quixotic generosity and a perfectly genuine desire to please, to 'make things pleasant', as one of his associates put it: his shadier activities generally benefited his shareholders as much as himself. He talked in effortful volleys, like a gun discharging with difficulty, and it was sometimes hard to understand exactly what he said: a straight question would receive a lengthy reply which, however seemingly sincere, would leave the questioner groping for its point. On the other hand, he had a firm grasp of detail and could make himself perfectly clear when he wished. Business matters were often despatched with a brevity that bordered on brusqueness. 'Your business must be ready cut and dried,' advised one who had had dealings with him. 'He listened, not always patiently or politely, but with sundry fidgetings and gruntings, to your story, gave you an answer in a few brief monosyllables, turned his back [and] took up the affair that came next.'

Born in 1800, the son of a Yorkshire yeoman farmer, George Hudson left school at fifteen and was apprenticed to a linen draper in the city of York. Though lacking charm, he made a good impression through hard work, and in the course of time he married his employer's daughter and became a partner in the business. When he was twenty-seven, a relative in Whitby left him an inheritance of about £30,000, an event which in later years he was to say half-seriously was the worst thing that ever happened to him. Without it, certainly, he might have remained a perfectly ordinary provincial businessman. As it was he became, by virtue of his suddenly acquired wealth, one of the most prominent citizens of York. He acted as the energetic agent for the local Tory candidate in the parliamentary elections, and he speculated a little in trade, not very successfully. A more significant enterprise was his leadership in founding the York Union Banking Company, which at once became one of the most successful provincial joint-stock banks. It was linked with Glyn's Bank in London, headed by George Carr Glyn, who was also a major figure in railways, as chairman of the London and Birmingham Railway then under construction.

In 1833, a number of prominent local tradesmen in York formed a Railway Committee. Their interest was stimulated by the success of the Liverpool and Manchester Railway and by promotions of other lines, particularly the Leeds and Selby, which would carry coal from the South Yorkshire fields to the Humber and, some suggested, might be profitably connected with a line south from York. On the face of it York was an unlikely centre for the infant railway industry. A proud old medieval city, the traditional 'capital' of the north of England,

it was being rapidly overtaken by such smoky industrial giants as Leeds and Sheffield. Its early entry into the railway race was chiefly due to its most ambitious citizen, George Hudson.

At the first meeting of the York Railway Committee enthusiasm was muted; the members were not sure what kind of railway they wanted, nor if they wanted one at all, until galvanized by Hudson. He announced his willingness to take up most of the shares and was appointed treasurer: during the early months of 1834 he tramped over much of the proposed route himself in company with the surveyor. At that time, a horse-drawn railway was envisaged, but a chance meeting between Hudson and George Stephenson, the beginning of a long and fruitful relationship, led to more ambitious plans. Stephenson converted the Committee to steam locomotion and gave Hudson the idea of a somewhat bigger scheme. Then at the height of his fame, Stephenson was already thinking far ahead, contemplating a railway between London and Edinburgh, via the Midlands (where the London-Birmingham was already going), Leeds, and Newcastle. Hudson would have liked to make York, not Leeds, the main link in this chain, but Stephenson saw more traffic in Leeds. Others, meanwhile, suggested a direct route from York to London but Hudson, influenced by Stephenson, rejected this alternative in the belief that a Midlands route was necessary in order to attract sufficient business; in the long run, this proved to be a strategic error. Hudson persuaded the York Committee to adopt a line which would join up with Stephenson's North Midland Railway, already authorized, running from Derby to Leeds. The new project was named the York and North Midland Railway. At the same time a group in Newcastle, with whom Hudson agreed to co-operate, was promoting the Great North of England Railway, to run from York to Newcastle. Thus York was shaping up nicely as the pivot of a north-south line from London via Birmingham or Rugby to Newcastle. The capital for the York and North Midland was originally set at £30,000. This was the period of the first railway mania and though local money was not abundant, there was no difficulty in attracting subscribers. York and North Midland shares were soon the subject of speculation since the £50 shares, of which only £1 had been called up, commanded a premium as high as £4, giving speculators a tidy profit. The bill authorizing the incorporation of the company and the construction of the line passed through Parliament without serious difficulty in 1836, and Hudson was elected chairman of the board. He was on his way.

As the value of York and North Midland stock rose, so did Hudson's personal prestige. In 1837 he was elected Lord Mayor of York, in which post he first showed that unamiable combination of lavish spending on official entertainments and severe cuts in administration, accomplished by reducing staff

York Railway Station in the 19th century

and wages. A free dinner for 1,400 York children on Queen Victoria's birthday hardly compensated for those unemployed or underpaid as a result of economies in local government. His fellow citizens, however, praised him for both his cost-paring and his banquets. He was so popular, in fact, that the York Tories succeeded in electing him to a second term as Lord Mayor despite the fact that he was not strictly eligible. This move, which infuriated his political opponents, is a good example of Hudson's tendency to make enemies unnecessarily. At one public dinner he quarrelled violently with the Recorder of York and, while rival supporters hurled cushions about, the two civic dignitaries were only with difficulty restrained from settling their disagreement with their fists.

One of Hudson's biggest beanfeasts was laid on for the opening of the York and North Midland Railway in the spring of 1839, an event described in the local newspapers at vast length in the overblown, sub-Miltonic prose affected by journalists at that time. Hudson spoke in generous praise of the engineer, George Stephenson. Stephenson replied with a speech that was to become increasingly familiar at railway dinners, dwelling on his origins as a farm boy and his early professional struggles.

A year later the North Midland Railway opened and, with the subsequent completion of minor links, it became possible to go by train from York to London (217 miles in all).

Meanwhile, Hudson was not standing still. He electrified the York and North Midland shareholders with proposals for branch lines to Whitby and Scarborough and, before progress could be made with those, he acted to safeguard the York and North Midland's control of east-west traffic by leasing the Leeds and Selby Railway, though at a stiff price. He would have liked to gain control of the continuation of the line to the port of Hull, but the Hull and Selby Railway refused to accept his terms. In reprisal, Hudson purchased a redundant steamboat company and reopened its operations between Hull and Selby to make life difficult for the recalcitrant company. All the same, he had to wait until 1845 to gain control, when he so far outbid the rival Leeds and Manchester, to whom the Hull and Selby directors would have preferred to sell, that the shareholders refused to allow their directors to reject Hudson's offer.

Already some more or less polite questions had been raised about Hudson's methods of accounting. Statements of expenditure were so vague that it was impossible to judge relationships between estimates and costs, while many items which might have been expected to occur as debits against revenue, such as fuel, insurance, and even interests on loans, were debited to the capital account. One shareholder diffidently suggested that professional auditors might be employed, rather than leaving the auditing to the directors themselves (effectively, Hudson and his stooges). The chairman was affronted by the remark. He had 'never heard of such a suggestion'. Immediately after this meeting the premium on York and North Midland shares rose from seventeen to twenty-four per cent. What better proof could there be of the excellence of Hudson's management?

The projected Great North of England Railway (York to Newcastle) had made slow and unsatisfactory progress, especially the plans for its northern half, and eventually its hard-pressed directors decided they could not complete it, opting for a line that went only from York to Darlington (opened in 1841). Hudson stepped into the breach with a plan of startling originality. He suggested that the eight established railway companies principally interested should combine to build and operate the northern half of the line, from Darlington to Newcastle. They should capitalize the project by offering to their own shareholders shares in the projected line with a guaranteed dividend of six per cent, which they would recover from the future earnings of the new railway. It was without doubt a creative, even inspired idea, always assuming, of course, that the revenue of the new line came up to expectation, but, not surprisingly, it ran into considerable opposition from the 'Liverpool interest' (a frequent stumbling block in Hudson's operations) among the shareholders. Their pet project was a route to the north up the western side of Britain via Lancaster and Carlisle, which a Newcastle-Darlington line would rival. Hudson's energetic advocacy overcame the objections from Lancashire, and he was elected chairman of what came to be called the Newcastle and Darlington Junction Railway, but that was by no means the end of his difficulties. An anti-Hudson publicity campaign of spirited invective was launched by the Stockton and Darlington Company, whose interests were threatened by the new project, while the Dean and Chapter of Durham demanded an exorbitant price for the section of their land that was required. Hudson neatly outmanoeuvred both – a jury reduced the Dean and Chapter's price by two-thirds – and in June 1842 the act was passed authorizing the Newcastle and Darlington Junction Railway. Hudson, according to what had now become his custom, secured the nomination of his own men to the chief posts in the company.

While the York and North Midland appeared to flourish from the outset, paying its grateful shareholders a dividend of ten per cent, the North Midland (Leeds to Derby) was struggling; overcapitalization, resulting from construction problems, was the basic trouble, resulting in negligible dividends. In August 1842 its disgruntled shareholders demanded a committee of inquiry, one of whose members was George Hudson. By virtue of his experience and his force of character, Hudson dominated the committee which, under his direction, proposed certain economies designed to produce, according to Hudson, savings in operational expenses on a startling scale. The directors of the company protested that the measures proposed, apart from forcing many people out of work, would result in such lowered efficiency as to endanger public safety. They received much support, but not from their own shareholders who, eager for the same kind of profit as the York and North Midland was apparently producing, backed Hudson. The board was reshaped, Hudson became a director, and his appointees filled the crucial posts in the company.

Hudson lost no time in putting his economies into effect, but the result was much as the sacked and discredited directors had prophesied. Such measures as the employment of children to work the points at junctions, the dismissal of employees who had lent their names to protests against Hudson's scheme, and the employment of inferior men at lower wages inevitably led to a disastrous decline in the service, for which sabotage, asserted by Hudson to be the cause of the problems, could not have been solely, if at all, to blame. An inquest on a passenger killed in a crash on the North Midland revealed that the driver at fault had less than one month's experience of driving a locomotive. Harsh remarks were made about Hudson and his fellow-directors, and the Board of Trade sent a strong letter insisting on improvements. At the next meeting of shareholders, Hudson was able to present an optimistic picture, though some observed that he had discarded the former system of accounting in favour of the simpler and vaguer methods he favoured in the York and North Midland: 'I will have no statistics on my railway', he is said to have proclaimed. A year later, moreover, it became apparent that Hudson's promises to slash working expenses and to boost the dividend were not being fulfilled; there were some savings, but they were roughly in line with what the former board had declared to be possible, a modest sum compared with that originally promised by Hudson; while the dividend remained around three and a half per cent. But by the time these unpalatable facts appeared, the shareholders were being carried away on a new Hudsonian tide of enthusiasm.

So far as Hudson was concerned, the acquisition of the North Midland was merely a step towards a far greater plan. The North Midland Railway, proceeding south from its junction with the York and North Midland, ended at Derby, where southward progress continued via one of two alternatives – the Birmingham and Derby or the Midland Counties, both of which connected with the London and Birmingham for the final run to the capital. Hudson's plan was to merge the three lines (North Midland, Birmingham and Derby, Midland Counties) in a single company. Due to over-capitalization, none of the three was doing well. In addition, the Birmingham and Derby and the Midland Counties were engaged in bitter competition, characterized by fare-cutting at a rate likely to bankrupt both before long, since both lines performed roughly the same function. The poor returns of these companies gave Hudson the chance to intervene between the directors and their discontented shareholders as a kind of divine umpire. The solution he suggested was amalgamation, but the Midland Counties, feeling it was in a stronger position than the Birmingham and Derby, preferred independence. Hudson then approached – in secret – the Birmingham and Derby, whose position was more vulnerable because its route to Derby was considerably less direct than its rival's. He worked out a plan for the amalgamation of all three companies, with an additional agreement that, if the Midland

49

Counties refused to join, the North Midland should lease the Birmingham and Derby Railway for seven years. That would have the effect of neatly slitting the throat of the Midland Counties, as the North Midland would naturally route its southbound traffic via the line it leased.

The gist of this secret scheme soon leaked out when the shares of the Birmingham and Derby Railway mysteriously began to rise. But the Midland Counties' directors still held out in face of the alliance of the North Midland and the Birmingham and Derby. Not unjustifiably, they felt that they were being exploited for the benefit, primarily, of George Hudson, and of the North Midland Railway. Hudson therefore appealed to the shareholders of the Midland Counties over the heads of its directors. To the directors he blustered and bullied; to the shareholders he presented a face of sweet reason. He produced figures which showed, he said, how large savings could in fact be made by amalgamation – for instance by the restoration of fares to a more rational level – and he expressed the opinion that the company ought to be earning dividends of at least five per cent. Considerable turmoil followed his speech; the Liverpool and Darlington interests were, as usual, reluctant to give in to Hudson's empire-building schemes, but the final upshot was that the amalgamation was approved and the giant Midland Railway sprang into existence. With this coup, the first major amalgamation of railways, Hudson emerged as a figure of importance on the national scene, and the soon-familiar appellation, the 'Railway King' (first bestowed on him, according to Hudson, by Sydney Smith), began to be used.

Hudson's kingdom continued to expand. No sooner had he completed his remarkable Midland stroke than he was deep in negotiations to extend the east-coast route to the north, buying up a small line in Durham on behalf of the Newcastle and Darlington Junction Railway, arranging financial backing for new companies to fill in the gaps between Newcastle and Berwick and Berwick and Edinburgh and to bridge the Tyne between Gateshead and Newcastle, stretching the York and North Midland branches towards the Yorkshire coast, and promoting an extension of the North Midland to Bradford.

By the end of 1843 the smell of a railway boom was in the air, partly as a result of Hudson's activities in the Midlands

FANCY PORTRAIT.

'*The Railway King*':
*cartoonists displayed
great ingenuity in
adapting the
characteristic forms of
railway structures to the
purposes of caricature*

THE RAILWAY KING.

and the north-east. These activities too were on Gladstone's mind when he set up his select committee for inquiry into railways, on whose reports the act of 1844 was based. The act, 'perhaps the most important milepost in the railway history of the [nineteenth] century'[2] was, as has been seen, intended to prevent the private interests of railway companies obstructing their obligations to the public and to protect people from

51

investing their money in unreliable projects, but, as it was finally passed into law, the act was far more considerate to the railway companies than the original bill. Hudson himself took a leading part in opposing the move towards state control, writing letters, making speeches, leading a delegation to 10 Downing Street, conducting private discussions with Gladstone (who was impressed by him, and notably remained aloof from the baying pack when Hudson fell), and to a large though unmeasurable extent his efforts brought about the concessions which, for practical purposes, made the 1844 act virtually a total victory for the 'railway interest'.

The whole controversy, indeed, showed just how powerful this interest was. To begin with, there were over a hundred directors of railway companies in the House of Commons. They could not of course be counted as a solid block, since they all had other concerns to take into account and in any case might disagree about questions of railway policy (most of the witnesses who gave evidence to Gladstone's select committee favoured some degree of state control of railways; even Hudson, at one point, said he would be prepared to accept it if it could guarantee safety from competition), but at any given moment the 'railway interest' within Parliament was larger than the number of those who were actually directors of railway companies. Gladstone himself cited his family's interest in railways as a reason for resigning from the Board of Trade. Then there were land-owners, who despite their initial hostility, were now anxious to sell off part of their estates at high profit, or acquire better transport for their produce (by 1844, opposition to railways from land-owners had become the exception rather than the rule). And behind the directors there was a whole host of people whose livelihood depended largely if not entirely on railways – agents, engineers, clerks, contractors, and, above all, lawyers. 'Most people have heard', wrote Herbert Spencer in 1855, 'how in those excited times [during the railway mania] the projects daily announced were very frequently set afloat by local solicitors – how they looked over maps to see where plausible lines could be sketched out – how they canvassed the local gentry to obtain provisional committeemen – how they agreed with engineers to make trial surveys – how, under the wild hopes of the day, they found little difficulty in forming companies. . . .' Railway business meant employment and profit for hundreds of solicitors and conveyancers, a powerful regiment indeed.

The 'proprietors' of a company were its shareholders, but the shareholders were an amorphous group, socially and geographically diverse, largely ignorant of business and with little practical influence. They might comfort themselves with the thought that they were safe in the hands of the company's directors since the directors' interests were identical with their own, but the truth of the matter was quite different. One basic problem of railway companies was that shareholders and directors (backed by all the people who actually ran the company, officials, legal advisers, and so on) had interests that were, or soon became, contradictory. To generalize, what most shareholders wanted was a safe investment that yielded a good rate of interest. Directors were usually more intrested in premiums, which were only to be achieved by expansion – building branch lines, buying up smaller lines or even moving into a different business, such as canals. In boom times it was not difficult to convince the shareholders that such expansion was worthwhile. For a Hudson, with his dynamism, his record of high dividends, his optimistic and unverifiable figures and his numerous other devices, it was generally quite easy.

The new project would usually be financed by an issue of preference shares allotted in proportion to each individual's holding – in other words, the major part going to richer shareholders, notably the directors and their hangers-on. Preference shareholders, with their guaranteed interest, did not care whether the new line made a profit or not. Moreover, as long as construction was going on somewhere, the company's capital account remained open, and it was an easy matter for the directors to use the capital account for expenditures that should have figured in the revenue account (which covered operating income and expenditure). There were, of course, legal provisions designed to stop such behaviour, but so long as the auditing of the accounts was exclusively controlled by the directors, they were easily evaded. As Hudson appreciated, the trick was to keep the shareholders reasonably happy and complacent with large dividends, which if necessary could be paid from capital. They were then unlikely to offer much resistance to new projects, on which he and his allies – and indeed all those privileged to know his plans in advance –

could make a fortune through premiums on the new shares. This system worked very well as long as it was more or less continuous. Trouble came when, largely through events beyond his control, the momentum was interrupted.

In 1844 Hudson's railway kingdom was huge – including over 1,000 miles of railway – and apparently impregnable; but appearances were deceiving. One potential weakness was that Hudson's system commanded no entry to the capital. Paul Johnson has remarked of rebellions in England that, without exception, they succeeded or failed according to whether the rebels gained quick control of London, and the same might almost be said of railway empires. Hudson's system depended on the London and Birmingham Railway of Carr Glyn. Their relations were close and amicable, but circumstances could change. Besides this, the route north via the London-Birmingham and Hudson's Midland conglomerate was far from direct. It was potentially vulnerable to competition, in the north, from the westward route via Lancaster and Carlisle (so far extended only to Lancaster), and in the south, to a possible direct line from London to York. At the very heart of his empire, a projected line from Leeds to Thirsk threatened to cut out the York and North Midland (Hudson's first railway and always his pet) from the main route north.

Hudson's immediate priority was to sort out affairs in the north-east, where there were a number of difficult problems to be overcome before a direct route from Darlington via Newcastle to Berwick could be completed. It was at about this time, according to his biographer, Richard S. Lambert, that Hudson, 'hard pressed by the growing complexity of his railway business, began to deviate from orthodox financial standards of conduct' (rather a mild way of putting it). He decided in 1844 to buy out the little Brandling Junction Railway which formed one of the links in the line south of Newcastle, and, having purchased it on his own account, he persuaded the Newcastle and Darlington Junction Railway to take over the liability. As the shares issued for capitalizing the deal rocketed, the Newcastle and Darlington Junction shareholders were grateful, and made Hudson a huge present of them (1,600 £25 shares). That little windfall apart, however, it later transpired that the total earnings of the railway during the weeks that elapsed before the takeover was authorized, amounting to £10,000, went to Hudson's bank without any deduction for the *costs* of working during that time. Another affair that was swallowed without question at the time but caused indigestion later concerned a purchase of iron. The price of iron in the autumn of 1844 was low, and Hudson was offered a large quantity on behalf of the Newcastle and Berwick Railway (not yet built) of which he was chairman. But his colleagues were unwilling to speculate, so Hudson bought 10,000 tons of iron himself. Three months later, when the price had risen and his colleagues had changed their minds, he sold most of it to the Newcastle and Berwick at a profit of £38,500. It is true that he might have made a larger profit by selling the iron elsewhere and also that the railway company would have had to pay the same price for their iron regardless of its source. Nevertheless, a transaction in which the chairman made a fat profit by acting as middleman in supplying raw materials to his company was, to say the least, open to criticism.

Meanwhile a serious menace, long lurking below the surface, had emerged into the light with the proposal for a direct London-York railway via Peterborough (subsequently called the Great Northern). This project had been mooted in the very early days, when Hudson had decided to throw his weight behind George Stephenson's preference for a line via the Midlands. Now that booming times had come again, Edmund Beckett Denison took the lead in promoting the direct route, most of the capital for which was expected to be raised in London.

Hudson devoted tremendous effort to thwarting this dangerous rival. From the shareholders of the Midland Railway he requested authorization to raise £2½ million to build three new branch lines to the east (i.e. into Denison's potential territory). He did not say exactly where the lines would run, nor would he promise that they would actually be built. As he put it himself, he asked for £2½ million, and got it, without telling a soul what he was going to do with it. He industriously gathered evidence against the Great Northern project, suggesting it was too expensive, that the gradients were too steep, and so on. He organized petitions and lobbied the Railway Board which, generally preferring established companies to new ones, came down against Denison's

RAILWAY RENCONTRE.

Since the appearance of our article, "The Battle of the Railways," letters have poured in upon us from the north with almost Niagarean velocity. The postman has reached our office in an almost fainting state ; and we do verily believe that, as it is the last feather that breaks the camel's back, so would one more letter have crushed the overloaded Twopenny. Our readers will no doubt remember our reference to a disagreement between Mr. Beckett Denison, M.P., and Mr. George Hudson, of high repute in the railway world, which, by the bye, seems to be just now the world in which every one feels an interest. It would seem that Mr. Beckett Denison exhibits the same extraordinary pertinacity in considering himself insulted, as was manifested by the illustrious Dogberry in having himself written down an ass. The honourable member evidently experiences a sort of satisfaction in being the object of an insult ; his feeling being no doubt akin to that of *Marworm*, when exclaiming, " I likes to be despised !"

An intelligent correspondent has favoured us with the following version of the affair as it actually happened. There is something of a dramatic tone in the proceeding, and as a scene actually took place, the form into which the facts are thrown is the most appropriate.

(*The Scene represents a Railway Platform ; Time, evening ; Passengers going to and fro, Porters, &c., &c.*)

Canon by four Porters, *coming forward with luggage on their heads.*

Air—"*Lo the early beams of morning.*"
Lo ! the early trains of morning
For us could no longer stay
Hark ! the evening bell is chiming—

Policemen.
Porters ! you must haste away.

[*The* Porters *go towards the trains. The* March *from* "Massaniello" *heard in the distance. Shareholders rush in, making gestures of joy and triumph.*

Enter Mr. Hudson, *singing.*

Air—"*Believe me if all those endearing young charms.*"

Believe me if all those extravagant lines,
They talk of so wildly to-day,
Were each made in the way its projector defines,
They're none of them likely to pay.
We should still go a-head, as this moment we do ;
Let Denison prate as he will !
When around me I see such supporters as you
I feel that he'd better keep still.

Enter Mr. Beckett Denison.

Air—"*When other lips.*"

When other lines in other parts
Shall in the market sell,
At premiums whose amount imparts
That Hudson chose them well.
When other minds achieve a task
My own could never see ;
In such a moment, may I ask,
Who'll ever think of me ?

[Mr. Hudson *and* Mr. Beckett Denison *greet each other.* — Mr. Beckett Denison *passes to a railway carriage, which he enters, when there ensues the following :*—

Mr. Hudson.
To make your line your capital you've got,
Though very long without it you remain'd ;
Although 'tis clear you would have had it not,
But that it was dishonestly obtained.

Mr. Beckett Denison.
Dishonestly obtained ! what mean you, Sir ?

Mr. Hudson.
Oh ! nothing personal, so don't mistake.

Mr. Beckett Denison.
You have no right on me to throw a slur—

Mr. Hudson.
Allow me an apology to make.

Cantabile. Mr. Hudson.
I said " dishonestly," 'tis true,
And to a public board referred ;
But meant not to apply to you,
Believe me, an offensive word.

Mr. Beckett Denison (*multo agitato*).
You said " dishonestly," and I
Believe you meant it to apply
To me.

Mr. Hudson.
I 'm sorry you should take offence ;
I meant the word in general sense
To be.

Mr. Beckett Denison (*con strepito, and pulling up the window of the carriage*).
I will not hear another word !
I 've been insulted : that 's enough

Mental Chorus of Passengers *in the same carriage.*
His rage is really quite absurd ;
He 's made of very peppery stuff.

[Mr. Hudson *retires from the carriage window, having found his efforts at reconciliation ineffectual, and* Mr. Beckett Denison *goes through several grand airs, which are not worth repeating here, and the Scene concludes with the following*

Song and Chorus.

Air—"*Scots wha hae.*"

Gents, who heard what Hudson said,
Gents who saw to what it led ;
Don't it enter ev'ry head,
He 's insulted me ?
Every day and every hour,
He, because he knows his power,
Always takes delight to shower
Insults down on me !

Chorus of Passengers.

If to passion you 're a slave ;
If a joke you treat as grave ;
Nobody his tongue can save
From offending thee.
Who from words as light as straw
Always will attempt to draw
Insults no one else e'er saw,
Must a ninny be.

[Mr. Beckett Denison, *annoyed at no one agreeing with him in the view he has taken, falls into a moody silence, and the train moves off.*

RINGING THE CHANGES.

Master Jones rang on Friday night several peals on seventeen different bells in Fitzroy Square. This he cleverly effected, without any apparent fatigue, by running from No. 1 to No. 17, and pulling the area-bells violently, one after another. The tones were very distinct, and a beautiful echo of each was heard in the drawing-rooms of the respective houses. Master Jones, who is only nine years of age, wound up his masterly performance with a grand triple bob-major on the visitors' and servants' bells of No. 18.

ELECTION NEWS.

As a proof of the importance which is attached to the Registration, we may mention that we saw at the door of a marine store shop, an iron grate having on it in large letters the word, "Register."

proposal in its report of March 1845, citing much evidence provided by Hudson. However, as it was Parliament which finally decided whether the railway schemes should be approved, Hudson had merely won the first round. The actual fight had hardly begun.

His next step was to confound Denison's plans north of York. Denison planned a connection at York with the Great North of England Railway, and in May Hudson suddenly acquired that company. The terms were extravagantly generous to the Great North of England's shareholders, including payment of annual rent some fifty per cent higher than the current total annual earnings of the railway. Even Hudson had to admit that there might be some loss!

The battle continued in London. The meetings of the House of Commons Committee considering the Great Northern bill lasted for seventy days – 'a saturnalia of obstruction and intrigue', as R. S. Lambert puts it. Hudson had no official standing, but that did not prevent him interfering. He spent, it is said, £3,000 a day solely on counsel who were employed to act as observers, pouncing hawk-like on any fault in the Great Northern's case and making it available to hostile witnesses. Hudson's tactics caused questions to be asked in the House, and the endless sessions of the Committee became a public joke. They did end eventually – with a tied vote. But the chairman gave his casting vote in favour of Denison's scheme.

Hudson was not finished, however. Parliament was nearing the end of its session, and Denison and his allies had to move fast if they were to get their bill passed. Hudson set one of his agents, a man named Croucher, to manufacture a spanner that might still be flung into the works. On House of Commons writing paper, Croucher wrote around to local postmasters to inquire into the standing of those individuals who had signed as subscribers to the Great Northern. The evidence he compiled became the basis for a petition to Parliament requesting that the Great Northern's list of subscribers be more closely examined, and the subsequent investigation revealed some doubtful cases: a pensioner whose income was 10/- a week, a charwoman's son who had subscribed for £12,000-worth of shares, and some similar cases. Such shenanigans were not unusual; in truth, the number of phoney holders of scrip unearthed was relatively small, but it was

A page from the humorous magazine Punch, *turning into comic opera a celebrated public row between Hudson and Denison at Derby Railway Station, 1845*

enough for the Lords committee to recommend a fuller examination of the Great Northern contract before the Third Reading of the bill was passed. That meant the whole business had to begin again in the next session of Parliament. Hudson had won at least a year's grace, and in the next session he was an MP himself, having been successful in a vitriolic by-election at Sunderland, where the Tory electors hoped, not without reason, that having Hudson as their MP would bring prosperity to their town.

Although it is difficult to assess his precise assets, by 1845 Hudson was a very rich man, a millionaire with some to spare. He had acquired several estates in Yorkshire, the largest of them apparently purchased primarily, if not solely, in order to block the advance of the Leeds and Manchester Railway into York and North Midland territory (he later sold some of the land to the York and North Midland for three times what he paid for it). He also bought a vast mansion in Knightsbridge, where he entertained everyone from the Duke of Wellington down. Wellington, now elderly, was not universally popular, due to his conservative politics, yet he was by far the greatest man in the kingdom; it was as if a Hercules or a Theseus were living at Apsley House. This great personage called on Hudson one day and humbly put to him the sad story of his sister, a lady of some years but no great fortune who had invested her savings in a railway company only to see the value of the shares diminish almost to vanishing point. Could Mr Hudson help? Mr Hudson would see what he could do. He began to buy shares himself in the ailing company, and as soon as word leaked out that none other than the Railway King was buying, the price began to climb steeply. When the Duke called again, Hudson advised him that his sister should now sell her shares, which she did at a profit. Was there anything the grateful Duke could do for Mr Hudson? No, thank you, but on second thoughts, it appeared that Mr Hudson's daughter Anne was attending a fashionable finishing school in Hampstead, where she was mocked by her snobbish comrades for her lowly background. Would the Duke be prepared to call to see her? The Duke would and did, and the effect of his visit was that the stock of Anne Hudson at her unpleasant school rose as sharply as the stock of the railway company when George Hudson began buying.

Hudson's help was not reserved for the mighty. He once advised an old acquaintance in York to buy shares in a certain company, but the man shook his head ironically, indicating that he had no money to invest in railway shares or anything else. Hudson said he would 'arrange that', and a few months later returned with a cheque for several thousand pounds, the fruit of an investment he had made on his old friend's behalf. For Hudson, making money had become as simple as making a pie, but this facility was in time to prove dangerous.

It is not surprising that he had a large band of devoted admirers. A testimonial to him to which grateful shareholders subscribed (alleged by his opponents to have been started by Hudson himself) raised no less than £30,000. Emily Bronte contributed £1, but her sister Charlotte forbore and wisely, though unavailingly, advised selling York and North Midland shares while the going was good.

In 1845 the railway mania reached its peak. Hudson saw limitless opportunities, but he also saw growing threats of competition. The Great Northern menace was never far from his thoughts, and he resolved to steal a march on it by a new venture in the eastern part of the country which would remove

One of Hudson's greatest moments: he ushers the Queen into the royal carriage. The Queen enjoyed the smoothness of railway travel and found it 'surprisingly quick', but was indignant at accidents to third-class passengers. A director should ride on every train, she said, 'then we should see a different state of things'

59

the need for Denison's trunk route. The instrument at hand was the Eastern Counties Railway, which in October 1845 invited him to become its chairman. The Eastern Counties Railway was struggling, its construction incomplete, its service notoriously poor, and its dividend sagging at around two per cent. Hudson, in taking it on and promising to make it one of the most profitable lines in the country, committed himself to 'an Herculean task', as *The Times* City correspondent wrote some years later, 'and placed himself amidst directors who had fairly exhausted their imaginations in devising schemes by which the company might maintain itself'.[3] There can be little doubt, as his biographer says, that this was 'one of the major blunders of his career'.

The Eastern Counties Railway had certain superficial attractions for Hudson. First, it had its own access to London; second, it might (he considered) form the basis for a new route north via Cambridge and Lincoln which could be portrayed as a better alternative than the Great Northern scheme. Thus, he could hope to lure away some of Denison's shareholders to the support of his own project. He set up a committee which met in a lawyer's office in Sise Lane ostensibly to discuss an amalgamation along these lines, though the committee's main purpose was to lobby against the Great Northern by all available means.

In June 1846 the long struggle ended in Hudson's defeat when the Select Committee of the Lords, judging between Hudson's Eastern Counties scheme and Denison's project, came down in favour of the latter. The Great Northern's act became law on the same day as the Repeal of the Corn Laws, another measure which Hudson, a devoted if somewhat unexpected Protectionist, deplored. Nevertheless, the Great Northern still had to be built – Brassey was organizing his men for the job – and Hudson could dream of clipping its horns by constructing railways of his own in eastern England. His energies were redoubled. At a meeting of the shareholders of the Midland Railway in May 1846 he outlined no less than twenty-six bills which he proposed to bring before Parliament, mainly concerned with the construction of branch lines. There were some demurrals but, well armed with proxies, Hudson easily won approval for all of them. A few days later he got the York and North Midland shareholders to approve a further six

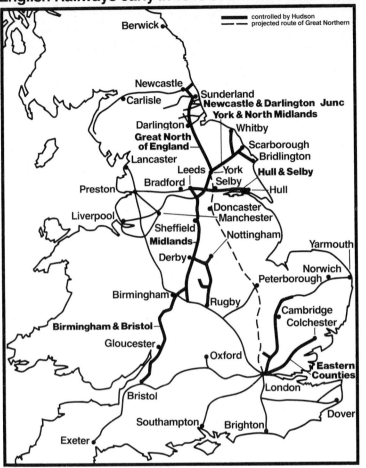

English Railways early in 1846 excl. some local lines

controlled by Hudson
projected route of Great Northern

Berwick

Newcastle
Carlisle
Sunderland
Newcastle & Darlington Junc
York & North Midlands
Darlington
Whitby
Great North of England
Scarborough
Lancaster
Bridlington
Leeds
York
Hull & Selby
Bradford
Selby
Preston
Hull
Liverpool
Doncaster
Manchester
Sheffield
Nottingham
Midlands
Yarmouth
Derby
Norwich
Peterborough
Birmingham
Rugby
Cambridge
Birmingham & Bristol
Colchester
Gloucester
Oxford
Eastern Counties
Bristol
London
Southampton
Brighton
Dover
Exeter

bills and the Newcastle and Darlington Junction shareholders seven more. Within the week he was on his way back to London by special train, having gained shareholders' approval for projects with a total estimated expenditure of about £10 million.

Clouds, small and not yet threatening, were nevertheless appearing on the horizon. At a special meeting of the Midland shareholders in July, Hudson proposed the purchase of the newly opened Leeds and Bradford Railway to prevent his old rival, the Manchester and Leeds (later Lancashire and Yorkshire), getting its hands on it. The Liverpool men among the shareholders stated in no uncertain terms their disapproval of the bland way in which their own chairman stood there

61

advising them to buy another railway *of which he was also chairman*. Their irritation was heightened by the provision that they should guarantee a dividend of ten per cent to the Leeds and Bradford shareholders when their own dividend was only seven per cent. Letters appeared in the press accusing Hudson of lacking both integrity and competence. Hudson might fume that it was all a dastardly Liverpool plot, but the criticism was not stifled. An additional aggravation, too, was that railway shares generally were falling in value: the Midland shares had lost about twenty-five per cent in value since the previous year; the Eastern Counties shares, in spite of higher dividends (which, it must have been obvious to anyone who paused to think, could not possibly have come out of higher earnings in the brief time that Hudson had been in control), had failed to rise as Hudson promised.

Recently re-elected Lord Mayor of York, Hudson still seemed to be king of the castle, and his banquets were grander than ever. He showed no sign of worrying that his railway monopoly was increasingly threatened – not only by the Great Northern but also by two big amalgamations. The first of these created the Caledonian Railway, and brought nearer the completion of a west-coast route to Glasgow. The second created the London and North-Western Railway, its two main constituents being the old London and Birmingham and the Grand Junction (Birmingham to Liverpool), and clearly threatened the alliance with Glyn's London-Birmingham line on which Hudson's Midland system so largely depended.

The Midland Railway was in danger of being cut off, north and south, and reduced to a provincial system relying on local traffic. The plans Hudson formulated in the summer of 1846 were largely designed to prevent this disaster. His attempt to gain an entry to Manchester was thwarted by the formation of the London and North-Western, but north of York he achieved a considerable coup against encroaching rivals when he formed a single company called the York and Newcastle by persuading the Newcastle and Darlington shareholders to exercise a long-standing option to buy the Great North of England, which of course necessitated a large increase of capital. In 1847 the Newcastle and Berwick Railway was added (the company becoming the York, Newcastle and Berwick), though the final link of the York-to-Edinburgh

'King Hudson's Levee'. Attended by a stoker, the 'Railway King' receives high-born petitioners; from Punch, *1845*

trunk route, from Berwick to Edinburgh, held on to its independence. In the south Hudson's plans were even more daring: in essence, they consisted of a Midland Railway extension down to Hitchin (on the route of the Great Northern) where it would connect with a spur from the Eastern Counties. This would have given his Midland system an independent entry to London. Although he gained parliamentary approval for both lines to Hitchin, his application to bridge the Great Northern at that point was rejected; the Midland and the Eastern Counties remained divided, and the whole strategy was ruined.

By 1847 Hudson's prestige was discernibly waning. Criticism of his empire and the way he ran it was growing, and a threat to make railway companies' accounts available for inspection by the newly appointed Board of Railway Commissioners was narrowly averted – Hudson speaking passionately against such interference. Economic conditions generally were becoming unfavourable, chiefly due to high food prices and the resulting pressure on capital. In the general election of that year Hudson easily retained his seat for Sunderland, but a tremendous quarrel broke out in York when Hudson forced a puppet-candidate of his own on the York Tories after, so rumour said, bringing pressure on the sitting member, Sir John Lowther, to resign. When someone moved the re-nomination of Lowther, the returning officer, a Hudson man, ruled the nomination invalid on dubious legal

63

grounds. Hudson had always had opponents in his home town, but his money and influence still rendered them powerless. All the same, it was costing more and more to keep even York safe in his pocket.

The depression already appearing in 1846 settled like a great wet blanket on the country in 1847. Money was tight: cash reserves in the Bank of England fell by half between January and April and were halved again between April and October; a number of joint-stock banks folded, and even the prestigious Royal Bank of Liverpool, despite a large advance from the Bank of England, was forced to close its doors. Railway shareholders had difficulty meeting the calls upon them to finance railway construction and the companies, if they were not to abandon the works, had to borrow money at alarmingly high rates of interest. Railway speculation was one cause of the financial crisis, though perhaps not the major one. According to Hudson, Free Trade was to blame: 'We cannot construct railways *and* import corn to a large extent,' he said, 'for in such a case the bullion will have to be sent out of the country.' Other defenders of railways pointed out, justifiably, that while railways might be responsible for fixing capital, even wasting capital, or making it temporarily unproductive, when railways were completed and in operation their effect was reversed. In addition, they provided a valuable economic stimulus, notably in keeping thousands of people employed.

By the end of the year the financial crisis was virtually over. Reserves were building up again and interest rates falling, but the economic recovery was jeopardized by political disturbances in 1848, when virtually every major European country underwent some form of revolution. Britain, except for heightened Chartist activity, was an exception, but trade was badly affected.

The difficulty of raising new capital meant that dividends inevitably were reduced and, as Hudson's whole system basically depended on keeping shareholders happy by large dividends, this seriously undermined his entire position. Poor trade performance in 1848 meant also that railway traffic, and thus earnings, were seriously depleted, for the first time in over ten years. It was unfortunate for Hudson that at this difficult time his unhealthy way of life – overwork and overeating –

caught up with him. He was ill for some weeks, and suffered attacks of angina ever afterwards. He had to abandon his daily visits to Billingsgate market where, very curiously, he liked to go to make sure of buying fresh fish. The death of George Stephenson, one of several old friends who passed on in this year, might have seemed to a more sensitive man an ill omen for railways. On the day of the funeral, Hudson was attending a Midland shareholders' meeting. The atmosphere was one of gloom, sparked by sharp criticism. Hudson, rattled, responded to complaints about the dividend with the remark that it would have been even lower than it was if he had not taken into account the probability of increased earnings next year – an admission that the dividend did not reflect true performance.

In the autumn of 1848 share prices of all railway companies fell sharply, Hudson's especially. The panic seems to have started when the public learned that Hudson had been compelled to repay some £400,000 to the banks, the effect of which was to leave the reserves of his companies dangerously low. York and North Midland £50 shares fell from £62 to £46, and others showed a similar depreciation. Hudson was ill again and his chief legal adviser, James Richardson, something of an *eminence grise* in the Hudson empire, was also incapacitated, with the result that the demands of angry shareholders, anxious to know what Hudson was going to do about their fast-vanishing investments, went unanswered. When it did come Hudson's reply was not very soothing. He forecast confidently that dividends would rise next year with greater earnings, but he based his forecast on the far from reliable assumptions that working expenses would comprise less than thirty per cent of receipts and that rates of interest would come down. Though the fall in shares levelled off, the shareholders remained in an angry – and inquisitive – mood.

At the half-yearly meetings of shareholders early in 1849 Hudson was expecting trouble. Rumours were abroad that he was thinking of getting out of both the Midland and the Eastern Counties Railways. The latter was clearly a dead loss, and the trouble with the Midland was that, with the intervention of the Great Northern, its future interests conflicted with those of Hudson's lines in the north-east. Since the Great Northern had to be accepted as a factor in the situation, the future interest of the York and North Midland and the York, Newcastle and Berwick clearly lay in reaching an agreement with it, which meant diverting traffic from the Midland.

The Midland shareholders' meeting was the first to assemble, and opposition was soon manifest in a proposal to appoint a Committee of Investigation into the company's affairs. This move on the part of the Liverpool interest was combated by Hudson, who still carried enough weight for his threat to resign if the proposal were carried to deter a majority of the shareholders from voting for it. The York and North Midland meeting also passed without serious trouble, but at the meeting of the York, Newcastle and Berwick, the last of Hudson's great creations, the going became sticky. Among the assembled shareholders was a London stockbroker named Prance who had been doing a good deal of homework, concentrating on the purchase of Great North of England shares by the York and Newcastle in 1846. He discovered that some of these shares had been bought at prices well above market value, and he rose to ask the chairman why the shares had been bought at what appeared to be an unnecessarily high price and, crucially, who was the fortunate person – looking straight at Hudson – who had benefited from the sale. To Hudson on the platform the questioner might have appeared as a chicken, a bird with a glint in its eye, the first of many coming home to roost.

Hudson was caught unprepared. He admitted that the majority of the shares in question had belonged to him and, in effect, that he had overcharged the company when the shares were transferred. He offered to pay back the profit he had made with interest, but Prance insisted that it was not just a question of money but of general principles. He demanded a Committee of Inquiry and the proposal was carried.

A week later the Eastern Counties shareholders met. Their chairman, however, was not present. He had sent a letter to the secretary, a former crony, using the excuse of a disagreement over some minor matter of policy to offer his resignation. The secretary implored him to attend the meeting, but to no avail; he had to face the music himself. Meanwhile, Hudson had arrived at Lord Stanley's London house for a political reception, only to be told that it might be better if he did not appear until the trouble at the York, Newcastle and Berwick had been cleared up. Society was already turning against him. At the Eastern Counties meeting, Hudson's letter was greeted with jeers, and the announcement that the half-yearly dividend would be even smaller hardly helped to improve the shareholders' temper. An investigating committee was set up under the chairmanship of William Cash.

Hudson's decline was swift. The recent events roused his enemies in the Midland. A few weeks earlier Hudson had used the possibility of his resignation as a weapon to force compliance; now, the shareholders were clamouring for it. The publication of Prance's committee's report, severely censuring Hudson, effectively ruined him. Suddenly, the Railway King found himself beset by a popular revolution. A couple of years before he had been the hero of millions, lauded in newspapers, the object of toadying flattery from his social 'superiors'. Now he was the object of near-universal detestation. The report of the Cash Committee finished him off. It revealed how Hudson had consistently paid dividends to shareholders out of capital, how Hudson and the secretary had run the company almost as if they were playing Monopoly (and cheating at that), 'making and unmaking dividends, traffic, capital, and revenue, just as they pleased'. At one point the other directors had become sufficiently concerned to set up a committee to look into the accounts. To this Hudson had replied, 'Well, gentlemen, I am chairman of this committee, and of course you will not meet until I summon you.' Needless to say, no summons ever came. There were records of payments to Hudson and the company secretary to cover various expenses, but no evidence that they had been actually used for the stated purpose.

Hudson still had a few supporters. *The Times*, in recent years a strong critic of Hudson, rather surprisingly defended him on much the same grounds that Hudson himself adopted: 'The system is to blame. It was a system without rule, without order, without even a definite morality . . . Mr Hudson's position was not only new to himself, but absolutely a new thing in the world altogether. His subjects exalted him to the position of those early kings who knew no difference between their own purses and the public exchequer.' It was pointed out

67

'*Off the Rail*', Punch's
comment on the fall of
Hudson, 1849

OFF THE RAIL.

that the shareholders were implicitly guilty of aiding and
abetting Hudson's cookery of the accounts, but that did
nothing to dampen the righteous indignation of those same
shareholders, eager for a scapegoat to blame for their current
losses. Hudson was compelled to resign from almost all his
directorships, and to repay money deemed owing to the
companies, such as the profit on the Great North of England
shares. In that affair his brother-in-law was implicated. Less
tough than Hudson, the unfortunate man drowned himself.

At intervals during the summer the various committees set
up by Hudson's companies issued damaging statements. A

typical scandal was that of the Sunderland Dock Company. In 1847 Hudson had offered to buy up any shares in this company at par, and as the shares were at that time languishing, a large number of his grateful constituents availed themselves of his offer, but while the shares were entered in the names of Hudson and one or two of his associates the cost of the purchase was charged to the York, Newcastle and Berwick Railway Company – apparently without authorization of the board. The York, Newcastle and Berwick committee turned up a number of equally damaging incidents. Money to pay various land-owners before the construction of the Newcastle and Berwick line had been paid from company funds into Hudson's personal account, for him to pay the land-owners concerned. But there was a discrepancy of £30,000 between the money going in and the money paid out which had suddenly been repaid to the company when the Committee of Investigation was formed. A somewhat larger amount had been drawn at various times by Hudson ostensibly to pay the contractors, but likewise had advanced no further than Hudson's personal account. Hudson's explanation of such discrepancies was unconvincing. He was compelled to fall back on the rather tired excuse that the size and complexity of his business had 'led to confusion'.

Similar stories were unfolded by the York and North Midland investigating committee. The company's accounts were said to be 'a mass of confusion', and for one period of eighteen months no accounts existed. The company was unexpectedly found to have an overdraft of over £100,000 at the York Union Bank due to 'various irregularities'. The committee published a list of twelve transactions of different kinds in which Hudson by more or less irregular accounting was alleged to have cost the company over half a million pounds.

He was forced to repay huge sums demanded by angry shareholders: the York and North Midland settled for £100,000 in settlement of all claims, to be paid in instalments, while others resorted to the courts. A libel action in Yorkshire brought by James Richardson against a local newspaper which, in discussing recently revealed misappropriation of funds in the York Union Bank, had remarked that Hudson was 'not only corrupt, but corrupted everyone round him',

69

resulted in a judgement in which the jury found no evidence of corruption (though it did cite 'artifice, mismanagement, and defalcation'), and encouraged Hudson to attempt a comeback. Rumours circulated that he had restored his fortune by successful speculation on the Stock Exchange, and that his help was being sought again by railway companies, but these efforts came to nought when it was revealed that one of his

publicity men had attempted to bribe the editor of a weekly
paper to publish an article defending Hudson.

The nation-wide bear-baiting was taken up in Parliament.
The Eastern Counties investigating committee had found in
the accounts under 'parliamentary expenses' a sum of nearly
£10,000 for 'secret service', and had petitioned Parliament for
an inquiry, the implication being that the money had been

used to bribe MPs. In the House of Commons, Hudson defended himself with a mixture of humility and self-justification. If he had been guilty of malpractices, he explained, they had occurred through error not design. Not entirely without justice, he asserted that 'the system' was to blame, not the individual. 'I think, if the House will determine what is capital and what income – what ought to go to capital and what ought to go to revenue – the directors would have no difficulty; they would be guided by the strict law of the House.' Apart from the odd *sotto voce* grunt of assent from his few remaining supporters, he was heard in silence; the air of disapproval was almost tangible.

Hudson himself had been brought down. The question was: how far should the investigations go on? Were his fellow-directors equally to blame, and what other interests were involved in the whole business of railway promotion? These were deep waters. The accusations concerning possible bribery of MPs prompted the House of Commons to investigate the affairs of the Sise Lane Committee, which Hudson had originated in 1845 to concentrate opposition to the Great Northern. It shortly transpired that a prominent member of that committee had been none other than William Cash, who had presided over the Eastern Counties' Committee of Investigation. A shrewd Quaker businessman, Cash had shown a lawyer's grasp of fact and innuendo when cross-examining Hudson, but when it came to the Sise Lane Committee, lo and behold, he could remember practically nothing about it. Predictably, the investigation into the murky activities in Sise Lane petered out. Cover-ups were being hastily devised elsewhere. The board of the York, Newcastle and Berwick came to an agreement with their company's investigating committee, the gist of which was that the directors should be allowed to retire quietly, leaving the committee to take over their jobs, all the blame for previous malpractices being ascribed to their former chairman.

Hudson remained an MP, a vital safeguard against the creditors now clamouring for blood. As an MP he could not be arrested for debt while the Commons was in session, and Sunderland remained faithful after even York had rejected him. But he was never at home in the House of Commons, and his abasement made it easier for parliamentary wits like

Bernal Osborne to capitalize on his ill-judged interventions in debate. Sir Walter Fraser related an incident when Osborne was speaking and 'the "Railway King" . . . attracted his attention by some inarticulate sounds, expression of doubts of the fact uttered by the orator: it was about six p.m.: turning upon Hudson, he said, "I must beg the Member for Sunderland not to interrupt me: at this *early* period of the evening he has no excuse for making a noise." This of course did not diminish the wrath of Hudson; who sprang to his feet; and endeavoured to address the House. Bernal Osborne, however, continued: "Sit down, pray! I accept your apology: say no more."'

Various suits in Chancery against Hudson eventually came to judgement with damaging effect on his character and disastrous effect on his finances. He was forced to sell his property; his Knightsbridge mansion was rented to the French ambassador. In 1855 he retired to Spain, partly to escape his creditors while the House was not sitting, partly in hope of promoting business there. His health, too, deteriorated.

In 1857 he reappeared in England for the election, and again succeeded in holding on to his seat, though with a greatly reduced majority. He was now a virtual exile, attending Parliament when it was sitting but jumping hastily on the boat train to France when it broke up. His wife lived quietly in a London lodging-house. Due to competition from other ports in the north-east the Sunderland Dock Company, for which Hudson had been largely responsible, was failing, and his popularity waned with it; in the general election of 1859 Hudson lost his seat – his last refuge in England. The death of his old associate, Robert Stephenson, a few months later gave him an opportunity to contest the vacant seat of Whitby, the town closest to his heart, the origin of the fortune which had set him on the way to his railway kingdom. But he dared not leave Paris and, failing to appear in person, he was defeated.

For six long years he moved from one French hotel to another, each one cheaper than the last, his condition scarcely preferable to prison. No new general election was held until 1865, and though already largely forgotten by the country at large, he had enough friends still in Whitby to secure his nomination as Tory candidate. But two days before the election he was arrested in his hotel bedroom on a politically

73

motivated suit by one of his creditors, and hustled into prison at – of all places – York. The Whitby Tories were forced to select another candidate in utmost haste; ironically, their last-minute substitute won the seat.

As there was no chance of squeezing any money out of Hudson, his creditors relented, and he was released from prison after three months. Some friends raised a subscription for him, enough to purchase an annuity of £600 a year, and he retired to a small house in London with his wife. Public indignation had now burned out, and he was kindly received on his occasional visits to the smoking room of that Tory mecca, the Carlton Club. In spite of financial stringencies and poor health, he remained cheerful and enjoyed talking, sometimes rather ruefully, about the past. During a visit to friends at York in the winter of 1871 he was taken ill. He returned to London, where he died a few weeks later. His body was returned to York for burial – by train of course.

There is no doubt that Hudson was a rascal. Whether he was a villain is less certain, and he was surely not a calculating criminal. Any feeling of disgust provoked by his career as a whole is likely to be directed equally, if not more strongly, at those who, having lauded and encouraged him in the days of prosperity when they were making a fortune out of his activities, turned so savagely upon him when his empire crashed, and raised their hands in horror, or their fists in anger, at the misdemeanours they had been quite willing to connive at when it profited them to do so. 'Why', asked Carlyle, 'should . . . the chief terrier among them be set upon by all the dog fraternity?'

Hudson had some sterling qualities. Charles Dickens, who had edited a paper in which Hudson was briefly interested in 1846, met a friend on the boat leaving Boulogne for Folkestone in 1863 who was saying goodbye to a shabby-looking man on the quayside. The man, who seemed familiar, was saying that he would not have a good dinner again until his friend returned to France. Later, Dickens asked who this poor creature was, and learning that he was none other than Hudson, the Railway King, inquired why his friend still kept up with him. 'Because he had so many people in his power, and held his peace . . .' was the reply. That at least could be said for Hudson. He never ratted.

3 The Contractor: Thomas Brassey in Six Continents

In the twenty years after 1830, when the first genuine public railway carried its first passengers, about 6,000 miles of railway were opened in Britain, much of it double-track. The material and effort involved was immense. Each mile of double-track, including sidings and various fittings, required an average of about 300 tons of iron. Michael Robbins calculated that in the peak years of 1844–50, when 4,000 miles were opened, approximately 12 million wooden sleepers were supplied for new lines alone (some replacements would also have been needed on older lines, the life of a sleeper being only about twelve years). Locomotives, wagons, bridges, stations had to be provided. But the greatest task of all was preparing the track, making cuttings, tunnels, and embankments to enable trains to run on direct routes and on gentle slopes, across marshes, over rivers, and through mountains. No organization existed capable of performing such tasks until the great contractors appeared.

It is curious that with all the contemporary interest in the early years of railway history, very little attention has been paid to the figure of the contractor. The engineers have received perhaps more than their fair share of attention: there is no lack of books on men such as George Stephenson or Isambard Kingdom Brunel (though Trevithick is a notable exception), but even the greatest of the contractors can hardly boast more than the odd, perfunctory biography. There are only two lives of Thomas Brassey, one published over 100 years ago, the other numbering little more than 150 pages. The contractor is, of course, a more mundane figure than the pioneering engineer, but the contractor, too, was a pioneer in his way. He did not, like Stephenson, have to prove that railways were possible, nor invent the machinery to make them so, but he had to undertake the largest construction jobs that mankind had ever embarked upon up to that time, overcoming a host of more or less unexpected practical problems in the process. The contractor also had to take risks at which any modern industrialist might quail. There was an unsubstantiated story told of a certain contractor who, examining a job before submitting his tender, decided that £18,000 would be a fair estimate. He talked the matter over with his wife, and on her advice rounded the sum up to £20,000. Further thought convinced him that he had better be on the safe side and call it £40,000. Next day, his wife remarked that he might as well make it £80,000. He did so, and still won the contract. As his original estimate was nearer the actual cost, he made a handsome profit, but the point of the story is that the situation might well have been reversed. He could have tendered £18,000 and found that his costs were nearer £80,000. In the early days there was no sure method of calculation, and even long experience did not always provide a reliable answer. One experienced engineer remarked that so simple a misfortune as an unexpectedly wet season, with all the difficulties that entailed, could increase construction costs by twenty-five per cent.

Originally, railways were built without a contractor. When George Stephenson was appointed engineer of the Liverpool and Manchester Railway, he did his own surveying, employed his own assistants and his own workmen. But, as the pace of railway construction accelerated, the sheer number and extent of lines required larger organization and more division of labour. The day of the big contractor had arrived.

Once a company had been formed to build a particular railway, an engineer was appointed to take overall charge of the whole business, to decide what works were necessary, and keep an eye on construction. Tenders were then invited to carry out the work. It might be divided into different parts –

sections of the line, a particular bridge, tunnel, and so on – but, increasingly, one contractor, perhaps in partnership with others, was appointed for the whole work or the major part of it. A big contractor like Brassey might be represented by agents responsible for different sections, or in some circum- stances by a single agent, and in that case he might never set eyes on the railway he was building. The contractor or his agent appointed sub-contractors to carry out various parts of the work – again, it might be different sections of the line or specific jobs in connection with it. Below the sub-contractors came the gangers, each at the head of his gang of navvies, the workmen whose powerful muscles shifted the soil. (The name 'navvy' was a shortened form of 'navigator', which had been bestowed upon the labourers who had dug the canals.)

The relationships within the hierarchy might vary. Big contractors sometimes maintained semi-permanent armies of assistants and workmen; others operated more flexibly – and more precariously.

The popular image of the contractor was shady. Many men who were, to say the least, ill-equipped to perform the job, were tempted to enter the business in the hope of quick profits. Stories of contractors drawing an advance from the railway company and later decamping with the navvies' wages unpaid were not uncommon. There was one case in Lancashire where the navvies, getting wind of their employers' plans to skip the district owing a month's wages, laid siege to their hotel, imprisoned them in the billiard room, and prevailed upon the landlord to refuse them food. It did no good in the end. The navvies were persuaded to let the two contractors out in order to attend the magistrates' court, but the magistrates could not enforce payment and in any case the contractors had no money – that was the reason for their attempted flight. Though fortunes – large fortunes – were made, a much larger number of railway contractors went bankrupt. Even Sir Morton Peto, Brassey's closest rival (and frequent associate), was ruined in the slump of 1866.

So great a personage as Brassey himself did not escape the aura of unholiness that hung about the contractor in the railway age. Arthur Helps relates how, on first meeting him, 'I was prejudiced and misled by the word "contractor", and expected to find in Mr Brassey a very different person from the

Thomas Brassey

one I did see. There entered an elderly gentleman of very dignified appearance, and of singularly graceful manners, suggesting at once the idea of what is called "a gentleman of the old school".'

Though Brassey was a self-made man, he had not started life without advantages. He came from an old family of Cheshire yeomen who, like all respectable nineteenth-century families, liked to claim descent from an ancestor who had come over with the Normans in 1066. When Thomas was born, his father owned two farms and rented a third, for £850 a year. The boy attended the local grammar school for four years, leaving at sixteen to become articled to a surveyor and land agent named Lawton. One of his early jobs was to assist in surveying the Holyhead Road, the famous coach road built by Thomas Telford. The railway age still lay in the future, otherwise no doubt Telford might have been content to construct a less massive thoroughfare; but it was good experience for a future railway contractor.

In 1826 Lawton made the young Brassey a partner and put him in charge of a new office he opened at Birkenhead. At that time Birkenhead was a small village, but its position across the Mersey from Liverpool, which in two or three generations had risen to be the greatest port in England after London, gave it potentials which Brassey seems to have recognized. He soon acquired other interests – lime kilns and a brickyard, bought with a loan from his father – while dealing in builders' supplies and acting as a land agent on his own account.

He entered the railway business on the advice of the man best qualified to give it – none other than George Stephenson himself, who met him while searching for suitable stone to build a viaduct on the Liverpool and Manchester Railway. Brassey's first tender, for a viaduct on the Grand Junction Railway, was not accepted; a lower bid had been made by William Mackenzie (a future partner). But soon afterwards his tender to build the Penkridge Viaduct on the same railway, between Wolverhampton and Stafford, was accepted.

The engineer of the Grand Junction Railway was George Stephenson, and his chief assistant Joseph Locke, a young man on the way up. George Stephenson, a tough, no-nonsense north countryman, possessed that quality so necessary for a pioneer in almost any field – the will to battle heroically against the complacency of ignorance. But as a surveyor he was sometimes inclined to be slapdash. When it came to laying out a railway line he was arguably less competent than some others, including his own son Robert – and Joseph Locke. At any rate, Locke was able to show that the tunnel to be built between Lime Street and Edgehill in Liverpool, started at both ends simultaneously, would fail to meet in the middle. Stephenson was affronted by this slur on his professional competence, and Locke was temporarily demoted. A subsequent error in Stephenson's engineering estimates, however, convinced the directors of the company that Locke should be appointed as joint engineer-in-chief. Stephenson, not unnaturally, could not stomach such an arrangement, and he resigned, leaving the meticulous Locke in sole charge.

Brassey's estimate for the Penkridge Viaduct, submitted to Stephenson, was £26,000. When Locke took over he considered this, and other estimates presented by different contractors engaged on associated works, much too high. He took the ferry to Birkenhead, put his own plans to Brassey in person, and invited him to revise his price. Brassey agreed, and his new estimate was close to Locke's own of £6,000. This was another example of the astonishing variability of cost-estimates in the early railway age.

The viaduct with ten miles of approach line was successfully completed, Brassey moving house to Stafford in order to keep a close eye on the work. From that meeting with Locke in Birkenhead arose a long and fruitful partnership and close friendship; they were later to share the rent of a grouse moor in Scotland. When Locke was appointed to rescue the London-Southampton railway from the mess in which the original engineer had left it, he invited Brassey to tender, and as a result Brassey was appointed to build the major section, between Basingstoke and Winchester, and later, since Locke warmly approved his work, other sections nearer London.

By the time the London-Southampton railway had been completed in 1840, Brassey had taken on three or four other contracts in various parts of Britain. His methods of operation were well established. In later years, he showed himself possessed of an unusual degree of that quality so desirable, though not so common, in a large employer, of delegation. But on his early works he kept in close touch personally, which

The Midland Railway at Penkridge, the scene of Brassey's entry into railway construction

79

necessitated many moves of house, a trying business for a man with a growing family, though his wife, whom he had married in Birkenhead, never complained: her support, and ambition for her husband's success, provided constant encouragement. In time he built up a team of agents and assistants in whom he placed great trust, a trust which seems to have been repaid with total loyalty. Samuel Wilcox, Brassey's agent for a contract in Australia, which Brassey himself never visited, was later asked by Brassey's son, 'Did Mr Brassey look over your figures?' 'No, I had to take the work before I consulted him.' 'He was absolutely in your hands?' 'He was indeed.' 'Did your correspondence with my father produce upon your mind the impression that you were labouring with and for a watchful employer?' 'I do not think it was so much that, as the extreme confidence he always put in his assistants. I think they could not help feeling that they had his confidence.' 'You would say, I suppose, therefore, that the stimulus with you to exertion in Australia was rather the feeling that you enjoyed the unlimited confidence of Mr Brassey, than that you were working under any kind of supervision?' 'Just so. I could not say too much in his favour.'[4]

Leading questions perhaps, yet there appear to be no instances of Brassey being substantially cheated by his agents, and few of his agents feeling dissatisfied with their own treatment. There was one case of a man believing he had been hard done by who brought a suit against Brassey, but he lost his case and in fact seems to have been suffering from a mild dose of paranoia. Brassey, who preferred to avoid lawyers as far as possible even if it meant some pecuniary loss, afterwards went to some trouble to find his discontented former employee alternative work. Brassey himself had a vast capacity for work. It was what he liked. He had few other interests and, like many successful industrialists, he was clearly not interested simply in making money. He advanced, or others advanced on his behalf, numerous more or less noble motives for his work: bringing the comforts of civilization to the rural masses, strengthening the sinews of the British Empire, stimulating national unity in a scattered and heterogeneous populace: Brassey might reasonably take comfort from contemplating these – as he supposed – desirable achievements. But what drove him on was the simple desire to build – railways, as it happened, though in another age it might have been ships or oil wells – augmented by an unquestioned belief in the moral value of hard work and material success.

Perhaps the most remarkable difference between Brassey's organization and a contemporary enterprise of comparable size is the almost total absence of a corporate headquarters – the vast echelons of receptionists, secretaries, publicity men, accountants, legal departments, and so on, so familiar today. Brassey's office was his house or his hotel. He had advisers certainly, like the lawyer, Wagstaff, his closest friend in later life, but until his last years, when illness reduced his capacity for work, he never had a secretary. His main filing system was his own retentive memory, and his correspondence was conducted by himself. In an age of great letter-writers, Brassey must have come close to the record in the sheer volume of his correspondence (not that, for the most part, it made entertaining reading), and it has been said that letter-writing was his chief hobby. When on the grouse moor with Locke, at lunchtime Brassey would retire to some sheltered spot, remove from a bag his writing materials, and get on with his letter-writing. Once after a busy day with a friend in Italy, Brassey stayed up in the coffee room to answer some correspondence after his weary friend had gone to bed. Coming down in the morning, the friend observed a pile of letters in Brassey's hand waiting for the post. Curious, he counted them: there were thirty-one.

Except for his agents' reports, Brassey was not much of a reader. Tolerant on the whole of the idiosyncrasies of others, he shared the common early Victorian feeling that reading was a frivolous pastime, all right for those who had nothing better to do with their time. There are even hints that he did not find it all that easy. However, faced with a sheet of engineering specifications, no one grasped the salient points more swiftly, nor made deductions more surely, and his mental grasp of complex calculations was legendary. One of his assistants recalled how he had been summoned to go over the prices on a particular contract. 'I noticed especially, after we had given him the cost, for instance of a bridge – all the details of the bridge and the total cost – he said, "How many bridges of that kind are there upon the line at the same prices?" Again, as to the culverts, or bridges of a different size.

After going through the quantities of the masonry, we went into the earthworks, and talked about the nature of the material and average length of "lead" from the different cuttings, and how much would this cost, and how much such and such a bank would cost, or such and such a deviation, and the prices of different parts of the works. Then we came to the question of rails: – they would cost so much delivered at the station, and so much delivered on and along the line. . . .

'We had to go into all these details . . . and then, almost in a few seconds, he arrived at the approximate cost of the line per mile, mentally.'[4]

His extensive correspondence notwithstanding, Brassey kept paperwork to a minimum. Even his agreements with sub-contractors were only verbal. Brassey would name a price for the job, and the sub-contractor would either accept or reject it. A written contract, he would say, was unnecessary: 'If a man is competent and has a fair price he will make the job pay, and accordingly won't try to get rid of it; if he hasn't an adequate price the sooner we make it right for him the better. On the other hand, if he's either idle, incompetent or troublesome, the sooner we get rid of him the better.' The last point seems to be the vital one, putting Brassey's attitude to contracts in a rather sinister light, but in fact his remark about making the price adequate was not pious hot air. Brassey was well aware that the cost of excavation, for example, could vary enormously: for one tunnel on the Salisbury and Yeovil Railway, the cost per cubic yard at one end was ten times the cost at the other end. Visiting the works of a sub-contractor and seeing for himself that instead of an estimated thirty per cent rock and seventy per cent clay the sub-contractor was encountering seventy per cent rock, he would make no bones about raising the price accordingly. It was said that he sometimes returned from a tour of inspection several thousand pounds to the bad.

Brassey believed in giving everyone an interest in the work he was doing, and for that reason he preferred the piecework system. A gang would be paid an agreed sum for a certain piece of work, the money being divided equally among the navvies, with an extra slice for the ganger. Within the conventions of his time, Brassey was a good employer, popular with the men. On the site, he would walk down the rows of heaving and shovelling navvies, exchanging a word here and there and greeting some old acquaintances by their first names – good labour relations on the part of a man whose workforce numbered thousands. (In 1850, Peto was employing 14,000 men – a larger number, as Professor Bagwell observed, than the New Model Army at the Battle of Naseby.) It was noticeable that when Brassey appeared among them, the navvies' notoriously foul language was abated.

Brassey did not care for trade unions, and asserted that there was no need for them since a union could not secure higher wages than he paid anyway. That was true, so far as it went and given the rudimentary state of labour organization, but it is noticeable that wage levels sank in times when railway construction slumped, to say nothing of the hardship of unemployment or the extreme hazards of the work; and in Argentina Brassey countenanced, or anyway connived at, the use of slave labour.

Brassey's entry into the business coincided with the first boom in railway construction, which by 1837 was petering out. Brassey was soon faced with what was to prove a continual problem for the big contractor – maintaining his organization during a slump. Fortunately, he was able to take advantage of the new opportunities which were arising not far from home, across the Channel in France.

Industrial progress in France lagged behind Britain, and the first public passenger-carrying railway there was not opened until 1832. By 1840 there were still only a few minor lines in operation, but the need for rapid transportation was daily more evident, particularly to connect the industrial region centred on the main coalfields in the north with the largely agricultural south which produced the food for the industrial workforce. Although France possessed most of the prerequisites for a major programme of railway building – national unity, political stability, expanding manufactures, etc. – there was a shortage of capital for investment, and largely for that reason the government in France (and in most other continental states) played a larger part in railway construction from the beginning. In Britain, free enterprise was almost total. Railways required an Act of Parliament – incidentally a time-wasting and expensive procedure which, according to Joseph Locke, could absorb twenty-five per cent of the railway

The magnificent glass-and-girders canopy of the Midland Railway's London terminal at St Pancras

company's subscribed capital – but the government exercised no control over where or when railways should be built. In France, the government invested part of the capital and also issued guarantees that encouraged the purchase of railway shares by private investors, thus acquiring a powerful voice in deciding what railways should be built. The national programme drawn up in 1842 (the year after Brassey signed his first French contract) envisaged a partnership between the government and the railway companies and government control of overall planning and of many aspects of management, including prices of tickets, standards of safety, etc. From the contractor's point of view the French system had certain drawbacks: one was likely to find a government inspector at one's elbow at awkward moments, for instance. The drawbacks, however, were outweighed by the advantages. Brassey himself much preferred the French system.

In Britain railways grew up higgledy-piggledy, wherever a group of businessmen were sufficiently motivated to band together and form a railway company. There was no national policy: some regions were served by several companies, often deliberately organizing their timetables so that it would be inconvenient for passengers to change to a rival company's line, and some regions were served by none. One effect of so many rival companies, evident to this day, is the large number of main-line railway termini in London. Thanks to the powerful advocacy of George Stephenson, discrepancy in gauge – a troublesome problem in several other countries – was less than it might have been, but on the Great Western Railway Brunel insisted on sticking to his broader gauge, and other companies' trains could not run on his lines.

Brassey used to say that French railways were better run, their carriages more comfortable, their stations more adequate, and their supervision generally more competent; but it was not only the passengers who benefited from the system of state control. In Britain, shareholders in the successful railway companies enjoyed large dividends; but there were many smaller companies which were less successful and some that were total failures, while the expenses incurred in obtaining the parliamentary act to authorize the Great Northern Railway equalled the total cost of building a sixty-mile line on the Continent. In France there was none of this; moreover, the dividends of French railways were hardly smaller than those of successful British companies. (Railway administration in France later resulted in some famous muddles, but that was after Brassey's day.)

Once the London-Southampton Railway was in operation, the advantages of a line linking Paris with the Channel coast became obvious, and the British directors formed a partnership with a Paris company to build a railway between Paris and Rouen, ultimately to link up with Le Havre. The two commodities lacking in France, capital and engineering experience, were largely supplied by the British. Locke was appointed engineer and, surveying the route, found no major topographical problems; but he was disappointed by the unrealistic estimates of French contractors, despite the relative cheapness of labour, and therefore proposed inviting tenders from British contractors. His suggestion was approved and Brassey got the job, forming a partnership with William Mackenzie, the only other British contractor who was seriously interested. Brassey moved to France – his wife spoke fluent French though he never learned it – and finding that it was impossible to hire experienced men on the spot, decided to import most of his workforce from England.

In the spring of 1841, Brassey shipped 5,000 navvies from Southampton and installed them in village lodgings previously arranged along the valley of the Seine. That was about half the number needed, but Brassey could not take more at the time as he still had various works going on in Britain. The rest were Frenchmen, plus a rag tag and bobtail of other nationalities: it was said that you could hear thirteen different languages on a stroll through the works. Englishmen were in charge, and the English gangers made themselves understood by pointing to the barrow to be moved or the earth to be shovelled, glaring at the foreign workmen, stamping their feet and uttering a few forthright '*goddams*'. It seemed to work, though in time a kind of pidgin English grew up among the gangs, mainly English and French with a sprinkling of words from other languages and a form of grammar all its own.

The navvies were a class, almost a nation, unique in nineteenth-century society, regarded with a mixture of awe, admiration and fear by the rest of society. Widely believed, without evidence, to be Chartists to a man, they were certainly pagans, and not very rewarding material for the few bold missionaries who ventured among them. Marching from job to job accompanied by their women – seldom wives – and living like some primitive tribe in mud huts, shanties, or in the open, they could be recognized by their distinctive dress, usually including a spotted scarlet neckerchief and corduroy trousers tied with string below the knee. They knew and cared nothing for established institutions like the Church or the Law; their wages were relatively high and were rapidly spent, usually on beer, of which they consumed huge quantities. They ate prodigiously too, especially beef, and believed rightly or wrongly that their diet gave them the physical strength they needed for the immense labours of earth-shifting they performed: like the miner in the song, navvies could shift sixteen tons a day and, like him, their wages were often mortgaged to the 'company store' or tommy shop. It took a year for an agricultural labourer to acquire the strength and knack to do a full day of navvy's work, a fact which was reflected in the wages he drew. Although such machines as steam-driven mechanical excavators existed, they were not widely used in Europe until much later. All the main railway lines in Britain, with their tunnels, cuttings and embankments, were made by men with picks, shovels and barrows.

The impact of the British navvy on the French was considerable. The local people, not surprisingly hostile at first, were softened by the freedom with which the navvies spent their wages, and the spectators who, filled with curiosity, made excursions from Paris to observe the railway works, marvelled at the sheer capacity of these primitive aliens. '*Mon Dieu, ces Anglais, commes ils travaillent!*'

The navvies themselves made few concessions to foreign customs. They retained their customary mode of dress, they scorned tools of French manufacture, and they demanded their accustomed rations of beef and bacon. They did, perforce, change their drinking habits, but found cheap brandy a tolerable alternative to English beer, no doubt with dire effects on their – already short – life expectation. They fought each other as often as ever, but there were no serious riots, as there were on the Lancaster-Carlisle Railway in 1846 – probably because the French police were better organized than their British equivalents.

One occasional cause of trouble was that the British navvies were paid at least twice as much as French workers. But then they accomplished more work than the newly recruited French peasants, and as the railway had to be finished in two years, they were twice as valuable. Every British contractor who ever uttered a word on the subject emphasized the superiority of the British navvy; it was an article of faith, like the superiority of the British navy, and in long discussions of the question of cheap labour, the conclusion usually reached was that the advantages to be gained from lower wages were more than offset by the slowness or inefficiency of the work. Foreign workers were amazed by the agility – and riskiness – of the navvies' method of tipping spoil down an embankment: a horse would be hitched to a wagon of spoil and whipped into a gallop by a man running beside it; as the edge came near, horse and man would leap clear and the wagon, running on, would strike a beam laid across the end of the track and tip its contents over the embankment edge. Strength, skill and daring were required and they were worth paying for: contracts usually offered large bonuses for completion ahead of schedule and exacted penalties for delay.

'Low rates of wages', wrote Brassey's son, 'by no means ensure low cost of work' and he gave an amusing example of the incapacity of inexperienced workers. When a railway was being built in Jamaica, all the plant and hardware required were supplied from Britain, including wheelbarrows. When the work began the local labourers, having filled their barrows with earth, raised them not without difficulty on to their heads in their customary manner to carry them away; 'and it was not without much expostulation that the English foremen were enabled to induce them to try the effect of placing the barrow on a plank, and wheeling instead of carrying the load.'

Although the Paris-Rouen railway included several bridges, and a tunnel over one and a half miles long, work went ahead rapidly. The navvies on this line, says Terry Coleman, suffered less than on many English railways, though their circumstances during the unusually cold winter of 1842 were grim enough. Work stopped, and so did wages. The streets of Rouen were filled with hungry Englishmen, and Brassey had to spend money opening soup kitchens and on other forms of relief to prevent his workforce breaking up. Compensation for injury was demanded by French law, unlike English, regardless of whether the accident was due to the workman's negligence, and a test case established that this covered British as well as French citizens.

In spite of difficulties, the line was completed ahead of schedule, opening on May 3, 1843, with great ceremony: bishops blessed the locomotives, and the navvies partook in a great open-air banquet at which oxen were roasted whole, under the watchful eye of a sizeable detachment of the French National Guard.

The success of the Paris-Rouen railway encouraged a burst of railway building in France. The company immediately began to pay dividends higher than British railway companies, with the result that capital flowed amply into France from London. Brassey had already begun the 300-mile Orleans-Bordeaux railway, where he entered into partnership with the burgeoning firm of Peto and Betts, and work soon started on completing the Paris link with Le Havre.

This was a much harder job, with many tunnels and bridges, including a great viaduct at Barentin comprising twenty-seven arches of fifty-foot span, rising 100 feet above the valley. There was an argument with the French about gradients; Locke, who was never afraid of steep gradients, advocating a maximum incline of 1 in 110, the French insisting on 1 in 200, which would have meant much higher costs and more time. A compromise of 1 in 125 was eventually agreed. By this time the majority of the workforce were French, though Brassey still sought his skilled workers – bricklayers, carpenters, miners (tunnellers) – in Britain. He was far from satisfied with his bricklayers nonetheless, and he

Celebratory dinner for the navvies on the Paris and Rouen railway, 1843, 'un repas . . . qui rapelle les festins des héros d'Homère', as a French paper said. An ox was roasted whole

was dubious about the quality of the local mortar, which he tried unsuccessfully to have changed. But work went ahead, from dawn until dusk, and in January 1846 it was almost finished. Various important persons came to admire the elegant Barentin viaduct, spanning 600 yards of space.

Early in the morning of January 10, one of the arches of the viaduct suddenly collapsed, and the remainder, domino-like, caved in after it. By great good fortune, no one was injured. Brassey was in Rouen, twelve miles away, when the news came. 'An accident like this would have quenched the zeal of most persons', wrote J. A. Francis not long afterwards, and Brassey, according to one of the sub-contractors, was very upset; but his reaction was characteristic – 'The first thing to do is to build it up again.' The reason for the disaster, and the question of financial responsibility, were less important. The worst aspect of the collapse was the likely effect on his reputation. Inevitably, much complaint and criticism had been uttered in France over the construction of French railways by foreigners, and there were many more or less influential people only too ready to say 'I told you so'; they accused Brassey, possibly with some cause, of attempting to go too fast. Perfectly aware of this likely reaction, Brassey endeavoured, in the long run, to turn the disaster to his own advantage, taking full responsibility and informing the company, 'I have contracted to make and maintain the road, and nothing shall prevent Thomas Brassey from being as good as his word.' The viaduct was rebuilt in six months, at a cost to Brassey of about £40,000. His reputation was enhanced in the eyes of the unbiased, and the line was actually opened ahead of schedule, earning the contractor a bonus of £10,000.

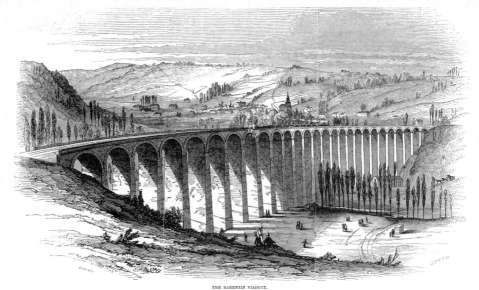

THE BARENTIN VIADUCT.

The distance from Paris to Havre, notwithstanding the numerous delays and stoppages on the way, was accomplished in six hours and a quarter.

The Directors, accompanied by their guests from Paris and Rouen and the authorities at Havre, then adjourned to a handsome dinner provided by the Company at the Hotel Frascati, where 200 gentlemen were entertained. After dinner, the Chairman (M. Lafitte) proposed the health of the King, which was drunk with all the honours. The health of the Chairman was then drunk by acclamation, and responded to by M. Lafitte. The next toast was the health of Mr. Locke, the principal engineer, which was drunk with great enthusiasm. Mr. Locke, in his reply, alluded to the extraordinary and vexatious delays in the opening of the line which had been caused by the Minister of Public Works and the Departments of the Ponts et Chaussées. He also referred to the extraordinary trials to which the works on the line had been subjected by order of the Government engineers—trials which were not only wholly unprecedented in the history of railways, but which were equally absurd and unnecessary. He pledged his professional reputation for

the fact that there never was a line opened to the public in a better working state, or the works on which were safer or more solidly constructed than those o the Havre Railway ; and he declared that there could not be a better proof of the solidity of these works than the fact that, though the Government engineers (whether from envy or a more laudable feeling he did not know,) had done all in their power to crush the viaducts, by laying weights upon them which by no possible future combination of circumstances they could be called upon to bear, not a stone had moved, nor a brick cracked, throughout the whole of them He then alluded to the extraordinary opposition which the Company had met with from the authorities of the city of Rouen—an opposition which showed much more selfishness than patriotism, and which formed a striking contrast with the slavish servility of the same persons when the question lay as to the making of a line between Rouen and Paris.

The only other toast given was that of Mr. Mackenzie, the eminent engineer and principal contractor for the works on the Line.

The train started for Paris again at ten

THE STATION AT HARFLEUR.

Brassey usually managed to confront setbacks unruffled. During the construction of a mildly disastrous line in Spain some five years later, exceptional rainfall created havoc. Brassey, in Bilbao, received a panic-stricken telegram asking him to come at once as a bridge had collapsed. Shortly afterwards another telegram arrived to say that an embankment had been washed away, then a third reporting further damage that demanded his immediate inspection. As he read this, Brassey turned laughing to a friend and remarked, 'I think I had better wait until I hear the rain has ceased, so that when I do go, I may see what is *left* of the works. . .'

Brassey maintained something approaching a monopoly of French railway building in the 1840s, until the 1848 revolution brought the value of shares down, and construction of new lines temporarily ceased. However, Brassey suffered no hardship from the French slump because the 'railway mania' in Britain, which began in 1845, had given him plenty of new opportunities on home ground. In the three years 1845–47, he signed about twenty new contracts with British railway companies, involving a total of over 700 miles, besides other works such as station buildings and an eighteen-mile line in Spain.

The 'railway mania' provided powerful support for Brassey's contention that greater state control, as in France, was preferable to the British free-for-all with its numerous shifty transactions; but he was able to rise above the tide of corruption and inefficiency by virtue of his pre-eminence as a contractor, which allowed him to pick and choose among contracts offered. It was Brassey who, with Locke again as engineer, built the Lancaster-Carlisle Railway, including a 900-foot climb over Shap Fell on a gradient – Locke again fighting off the protests of the timid – which for one stretch of four miles climbed at the rate of 1 in 75.

Proposed railways frequently had to overcome intense opposition of a more general kind than arguments over gradients. It was contesting various forms of opposition – some of it environmental, like Wordsworth's protest against the railway through the Lake District, some of it from rival railway companies – which accounted for the great expense of getting the enabling act through Parliament. The Great Northern Railway, Brassey's major contract of the late 1840s,

Scenes from the opening of the Rouen and Havre Railway in 1847. The illustration at the top shows Brassey's elegant Barentin viaduct, rebuilt after the disastrous collapse of January 1846

provided an example of the difficulties that railway promoters faced from their opponents.

The desirability of a direct north-south line on the eastern side of the country, linking London and York, seemed obvious enough, but it was opposed by two of the major railway interests in Britain, who feared the competition it would offer. Currently, the main route from York to London was via George Hudson's Midland lines to Birmingham, and thence via the London and North-Western of Carr Glyn, a powerful banker, and his intimidating general manager, Captain Mark Huish. More powerful opponents than these could not have been found. However, the chief promoter of the Great Northern was a no less formidable personality, Edmund Beckett Denison, the wealthy MP for Doncaster, who possessed more than the normal amount of Yorkshire stubbornness and determination.

One of the first casualties of the battle was Locke, who had been appointed engineer to the Great Northern. He resigned, for reasons that remain mysterious. He had often been employed by Glyn's London and North-Western Company, and Hudson too may have uttered a word of warning; at any rate, as no other explanation can be readily found, it seems likely that some more or less disreputable pressure was brought to bear. Locke's defection, however, was not a serious drawback. According to legend, Denison heard of the resignation late one evening. He immediately called for his horse and rode to the house of William Cubitt, later Sir William and head of a great engineering dynasty. Arriving in the middle of the night, Denison hammered vigorously on the door until at last an upper window opened and Cubitt himself, wearing a nightcap, leaned out to inquire what the noise was about. Denison offered him the position of engineer-in-chief, and Cubitt at once accepted.

Meanwhile, the struggle to get the requisite bill through Parliament continued. A subcommittee of the House of Commons debated the matter for three months, hearing reams of evidence for and against. The Great Northern Company and its allies ultimately spent the mind-boggling sum of £433,000 on securing their act: nearly half a million spent and not a shovelful of earth yet moved.

Brassey also suffered from the Great Northern's teething

problems. The first part of the line which he built, from London to Peterborough, proved unexpectedly difficult; he had a very tight schedule and a penalty clause in his contract of £5,000 per month. When the 'railway mania' collapsed in the autumn of 1847, credit dried up almost completely, and the company having been forced to spend so much of its capital in obtaining the Act of Parliament, work would have come to a standstill if Brassey had not agreed – he had little alternative unless he was to disband his workforce – to accept payment in bonds. Although the bonds were eventually redeemed, Brassey lost money overall.

The part of the line which caused the most trouble was the three-mile section crossing Whittlesea mere, near Peterborough, a bog twenty-two feet deep where, as Brassey said, if you stamped your foot a whole acre quivered. He was not sure how the mere was to be crossed until he found the method by one of those strokes of luck which were a minor feature of his career. He was discussing the problem one day in a railway carriage with an acquaintance who, gesturing to the man seated next to him, said, 'You had better get Mr Ballard's advice.' This man, an engineer on the Bedford Middle Level in the Fens, provided the answer. Ballard's advice was to make a platform of faggots, place a layer of peat on top, then lay another platform of faggots, add a covering of more peat, and so on. The platform was floated into position, and soil piled gradually on top, making it sink downwards so gently that the water was driven out but the more solid material remained – like squeezing a sponge. A somewhat similar method was proposed for stabilizing the piers of bridges in this marshy country. Brassey promptly appointed Ballard his agent for this part of the works, and his methods proved highly successful.

The collapse of the 'railway mania' brought harder times. Contracts in Britain dwindled almost to nothing – Brassey contracted for a few short lines only in the years 1848–50 – but once again he found employment abroad, in Spain, Italy, the Netherlands, Scandinavia, and in France, where Louis Napoleon entertained him to dinner and awarded him the cross of the Legion of Honour. 'Mrs Brassey will be pleased to have it,' the contractor remarked simply: there was no affectation in his indifference to titles and honours. He became increasingly involved in financing railways with which he was associated, and made some shrewd investments in land in places where he foresaw railways raising land values. He also made some mistakes.

In 1852, Brassey, in partnership with Peto and Betts, contracted to build the Grand Trunk Railway of Canada. It was to run 539 miles – at that time the longest railway in the world – from Quebec to Toronto along the valley of the St Lawrence, crossing the river by the Victoria Bridge at Montreal. One of the biggest projects with which Brassey was ever connected, it was also the least successful and the one which brought more criticism upon him than anything else in his long career as a railway builder.

The purpose of the Grand Trunk Railway was to provide reliable, year-round transportation on eastern Canada's main transportation route. The river itself is frozen and therefore unnavigable for half the year, and at the best of times ocean-going ships could go no farther than Lake Ontario. The Grand Trunk was eventually to provide direct communication between Rivière du Loup (east of Quebec) and Detroit. For more than half its length the railway was to pass through unsettled country, much of it heavily forested. The line would encourage settlement, it would help in fostering a sense of national unity among the Canadian provinces, and it would stop the drain of Canadian goods southward to New York, via US railways, which was impoverishing Canadian ports.

The mistakes of the contractors and promoters of the Grand Trunk Railway arose from over confidence, unfamiliarity with local conditions, from understandable though unfor-tunate decisions which might have worked perfectly in different circumstances, and from bad luck. There was from the first a good deal of criticism in Canada, part of it arising from the feeling that Canadian railways ought to be built by Canadians, and exacerbated by the lavish expenditure on promotion by the London-based company which later came cap in hand for more money. The whole affair was to cause long-lasting bitterness.

Finances were unsound. Brassey and Peto confidently foresaw large profits, and when the British government dashed the rather sanguine hopes of many by declining to support the enterprise, the contractors offered to raise the money in exchange for the contract. The estimated price of the railway was close on £10 millions or about £20,000 a mile, exceedingly high by current standards; but the eventual cost was half as much again. The London bankers Glyn and Baring, the leading financiers, insisted that only some of the capital should be subscribed to begin with; some £2 million of so-called 'B' stock was to be held by the contractors for eventual sale to 'A' stock holders. This assumed that the railway was successful; if it were not, the contractors were likely to be left with £2 million of worthless paper, which is more or less what happened. Thus the capital for construction of the railway was not all available at the outset and, if it were to keep flowing, the railway had to show signs of profitability. The original capital, moreover, was subject to severe and immediate drains. It was necessary to spend no less than £$2\frac{1}{4}$ million to buy out A. T. Galt, a Canadian contractor who owned various important concessions on parts of the route and drove a hard bargain; while interest on loans had to be paid out of capital until the railway began to operate – for several years as things turned out.

Arguments over the route of the railway really boiled down to two notions: a grand trunk route running straight through, or a system of local lines, built one by one, directly serving various communities in a much wider area. Although the latter system, preferred by Galt, could have been completed ultimately by local contractors, political considerations favoured the former, which required much larger operators. The grand trunk route, however, was to prove a failure: it had poor access to St Lawrence ports, it by-passed many large or growing towns, and it encountered fierce competition from the shipping companies of the Great Lakes and the St Lawrence. Moreover, a most unfortunate decision was made in favour of a broad gauge, with the result that the Canadian railway could not connect with the United States lines except by time-consuming and costly trans-shipment at the linking terminals.

The line was divided into four sections, each under a different agent, and another bold but mistaken decision was to embark on all four sections simultaneously. Had they been built consecutively, the enormous problems of labour and supply (the navvies' food, for example, had to be transported through the wilderness) would have been greatly reduced, and

95

the railway would have started earning while the later sections were still under construction. A more adequate survey also might have been undertaken. In spite of the presence of Robert Stephenson as consulting engineer, some sections were planned merely on the basis of what one man could judge with the unaided eye from the saddle of a horse. As a result, some unexpectedly steep gradients and sharp curves had to be incorporated, which led to higher costs of operation.

The labour problems might have been more easily foreseen. There was such a shortage of labour in Canada that Brassey shipped out 3,000 workmen from Liverpool; in Canada he had to pay them half again as much in wages as they earned in Britain. Later, he advocated bringing in gangs of French Canadians, paying a bonus to the gangers for each man recruited. The French Canadians, though keen enough, were lightweights compared to the British navvies and were only capable of working with frequent breaks; Brassey's agent put this down to insufficient meat in their diet. Conditions anyway made it difficult to perform the same amount of work per day as in Europe. The men lived in grim little huts – there was no possibility of billeting them upon the local population, the system Brassey preferred, because the population along most of the route was non-existent. It was so cold that little work could be done from November to May, in the depth of the winter none at all. The navvies worked in thick, incapacitating clothing, in temperatures far below freezing. Frostbite was a danger and at one time an outbreak of cholera reduced the workforce by one-third. There were more strikes than Brassey was accustomed to, and many of the British workers gradually drifted away. In the United States, labour-saving machines of various types had been extensively used in railway construction, and a steam-driven excavator was used on the Grand Trunk. The British agents, however, were not keen on it, finding it at best a way of overcoming the labour shortage, no less expensive than manual labour.

Besides labour, most of the plant had to be imported. Brassey established the Canada Works at his old stamping ground of Birkenhead, which made all the rolling stock, ironwork for bridges, and some tools, but there were obvious disadvantages in having the factory 3,000 miles away from the site. Apart from the expense of transportation, the problem of

Laying the track of the Grand Trunk Railway of Canada on the Victoria Bridge, Montreal. This was the first major stretch of what in the course of time became the Canadian-Pacific; from a photograph taken in 1859

getting the right part to the right place at the right time was not always overcome. Money apart, the products of the Canada Works were made to a high standard, and we hear of one of the iron tubes for the Victoria Bridge containing 10,000 pieces of metal and half a million rivet holes of which not a hole had to be redrilled, so minutely exact was the work. On the other hand, we hear, too, of the failure of a British-made steam-driven transporter, for carrying stone from the quarry to the bridge site; the men on the spot knocked together a better one.

The whole enterprise was conceived on too grand a scale. Brassey once said that he expected anything he built to be in good shape a century later, and as a rule he built accordingly. He followed the same methods in Canada as in Europe, but while some American machine tools were used at the Canada Works, he might have altered his ideas with advantage if he had made a preliminary inspection of railroads in the United States. American railroads were on the whole poorer in quality (hence the invariable use of 'bogies' on locomotives), and there was a greater emphasis on speed and cheapness. US engineers

97

excelled in labour-saving machinery and in simplifying structures. Their bridges were lightweight constructions of strut and trellis – a far cry from the monumental Victoria Bridge, which was one and three quarter miles long, took over five years to build, and cost £2 million. It was a magnificent bridge, too magnificent for the circumstances.

Within two years the Grand Trunk Railway was in financial trouble. Surviving capital was hardly enough to cover interest payments, and that situation prevented the sale of shares. Pressure was brought to bear on the reluctant Canadian government, which lent about £3 million and guaranteed the interest on share capital – a liability of about £500,000 a year for ninety-nine years. Brassey paid his one visit to North America in connection with this matter, landing at New York and travelling north in something like a triumphal progress. Special carriages were added to trains for his benefit, and he was accompanied by the managers of the railway companies on whose lines he travelled. He was vastly interested in the sights pointed out to him, especially the great grain elevators and, of course, the railways themselves. He came to appreciate that in America the railway was not so much a link between long-established centres of civilization as itself the pioneer of civilization, in many places built where no roads ran and no houses stood. He liked the system of allotting land by the side of railways to the promoters of the line, a custom by which he later benefited in Argentina.

Though it was finally completed, the Grand Trunk Railway was not a success. The company had difficulty in obtaining and maintaining rolling stock and staff, and traffic was always disappointing. The disillusioned Canadians felt they had been exploited by the promoters, who had left them no real alternative but to support the near-bankrupt line with grants and loans. On the other hand, few people made a profit out of the business, certainly not the contractors. Brassey's losses were not precisely calculable, but certainly large: a figure of £1 million was mentioned. It is doubtful how much blame should be apportioned to him personally. He had certainly gone too blithely into the project, anticipating large profits, and it was not the only occasion on which he was accused of exploitation. In February 1850 the London *Times* reported a circular to the shareholders of the Caledonian

Railway, issued by its London committee, which suggested that the terms of the contract entered into by Brassey to work the line, which at that time was in some difficulty, were far too generous to him. Brassey's response was aggrieved. In tones of sorrow more than anger, he at once submitted his resignation to the board of directors. It appears that the London committee was too hasty, for according to O. S. Nock, Brassey was 'proposing to do the job at the slenderest of profit margins, fully aware of the risks involved'.

In the case of the Grand Trunk Railway he could hardly be accused of avarice, in view of results, though he could be accused of failing to take account of the problems that would be encountered. One of the few faults attributed to him by his admiring biographers is that he always found it difficult to say no. Many close friends and associates were involved in the Grand Trunk Railway. Although there is no evidence that he had any private misgivings at the outset, this was a contract that he would have done better to have refused.

Early in 1854, Britain and France, as allies of Turkey, sent forces to the Black Sea to attack the Russians in the Crimean War. The British commander-in-chief was Lord Raglan, who had last seen active service at Waterloo and had an unfortunate tendency to refer to the enemy as 'the French'. Other aspects of the campaign were similarly ill-prepared. After some initial dithering, the object of the expedition was declared to be the capture of Sebastopol, and in September the allied armies landed on the coast of the Crimean peninsula with the aim of capturing the city before winter. The Russians had been given plenty of time to reinforce it, and though they are said to have lost two-thirds of their forces on the way, it soon became clear that a substantial siege would be necessary. It was not, however, the Russian forces that presented the major difficulty. The allied armies were absurdly ill-clothed and ill-equipped, and were soon ravaged by cholera. As grim winter approached, their desperately needed supplies were reduced to a trickle.

Although the British lines were only about six miles as the crow flies from the nearest landing place at Balaklava, there was no proper road, the British neglected to build one, and the unsurfaced tracks soon degenerated into muddy, rutted troughs impassable for any wheeled vehicle. It was much easier to get supplies from England to the Black Sea than it was to get them the last few miles overland. News of the grim state of the army reached London via the despatches of W. H. Russell of *The Times*, and the contractors stepped forward to do their bit. The lead was taken by Sir (as he was soon to become) Morton Peto, in partnership with his brother-in-law Edward Betts and his partner on the Canadian Grand Trunk and other railways Thomas Brassey. Peto was an MP who, according to his own account was approached by the Duke of Newcastle on behalf of the government, though from other reports it appears that the original idea was Peto's own. At any rate, Peto and his associates volunteered to build a railway from Balaklava up the steep ridge to the British camp south of Sebastopol. They would provide the labour, the equipment and rolling stock, they would operate the line when it was built, and they would take no profit. The government accepted thankfully.

In his London office, Betts, the chief organizer, was flooded out with eager applicants; the pay was good, but some of the navvies seemed chiefly attracted by the idea of taking part in a war. Frequently the object of popular admiration, though always mixed with moral disapproval and a dash of fear, the navvy became the hero of the hour. Others too seemed to have the thought that his presence in the Crimea would have a more immediate effect on the battle than the provision of better transport. 'If ever these men come to hand-to-hand fighting with the enemy', mused the *Illustrated London News*, 'they will fell them like ninepins.' The equipment – fairly lavish – with which the navvies were provided included a number of revolvers, a frightening thought for those who had observed their propensity to fight among themselves. There were predictable riots in Gibraltar on the way out, and strikes on the job; the work was accomplished with amazing speed nonetheless.

Twenty-three ships, many supplied by a steamship company run by Peto and Brassey, were needed to transport the workforce and its equipment – 500 men, fifty horses, rails, sleepers, tools, wagons, etc. Brassey advised the engineer in charge, a man named Beattie who had served on the Grand Trunk of Canada and was to kill himself by overwork in the Crimea, not to be too particular about standards; speed was essential, security and permanence less vital. Indeed, it was a

SPADES ARE TRUMPS.

Navvy (to Ab—rd—n). "NOW, OLD STICK-IN-THE-MUD, LET *ME* TRY IF I CAN GET YOU OUT OF THE MESS."

poor railway by comparison with civilian lines. No locomotives were planned originally, though some went out
later; the wagons, which were old and in some cases required
extensive repairs before they could be put to work, were to be
drawn by horses where the line was level, and by cable,
powered by a stationary steam engine, up the steep gradients.

It was not the first war-time railway. Though British officers
were suspicious of it – what had been good enough for
Wellington was good enough for them – a good deal of thought
had been given to the possible functions of railways in war-time
by writers in Germany and France; the Prussians had used

*The navvy to the rescue:
Lord Aberdeen and his
generals about to be
extracted from the
Crimean mire by the
spades of the railway
men*

101

railways advantageously in their quarrel with the Danes (when both sides, to Brassey's annoyance, also used the men and equipment he was employing to build railways in Denmark at the time).

The results of the Crimean Railway silenced doubts. A long section of the line was in use within six weeks of the navvies' landing at Balaklava; eventually thirty miles (forty counting double track) were built, including the branch lines that supplied different parts of the front. The capacity was said to be 700 tons a day. Though of course a much smaller enterprise, the contractors had shown that they were far more competent at building and operating a railway than the generals were at running a campaign. The work was not done without friction; it provided an early example of the recurring difficulties that arise when a totally civilian enterprise (the contractors had insisted on that: the navvies were called the Civil Engineering Corps) operates in a military context. Embarrassment could arise from the fact that the navvies were better paid than the soldiers, while the strategy of generals often tends to conflict with the plans of contractors. In the end, though, the military paid fair tribute to the railway men. General Burgoyne admitted that it was impossible to overrate the effect of the railway in shortening the siege (which ended with the fall of Sebastopol in September 1855), and Captain Clifford remarked in a letter home that the navvies 'do more work in a day than a Regiment of English soldiers do in a week'.

In the late 1850s Brassey found large profits harder to come by. In Britain he was taking on as many contracts as ever, but they were nearly all for comparatively short lines, less attractive to a big operator, as most of the major lines were already built. He did well in France and Italy, and in 1856 he signed his first contract for an Austrian railway; it was a small one but important for Brassey because it established him in what was to be a fruitful region in the future. Two years later he agreed to build the Eastern Bengal Railway. He had declined earlier opportunities for railway construction in India as he had doubts about its profitability, doubts which would seem to have been well-founded in view of the losses he incurred on the Eastern Bengal Railway. Nevertheless, Brassey as a devoted imperialist found the prospects in India

inviting (he could not have foreseen that the sense of unity encouraged by better communications would find expression in Indian nationalism rather than loyalty to the British Empire), and later contracts in India were sweetened by a government guarantee of five per cent to the contractors on top of costs – an arrangement which made it virtually impossible to lose money. There was some criticism of the high prices paid for Indian railways, though if they were to be built quickly and well they could probably not have been built more cheaply.

The famous Crimean railway was not very well built and not very up-to-date (horses were used at first to draw the wagons), but it nevertheless excited much local interest

In Australia, as in Canada, shortage of labour was the major problem, and in 1859 Brassey shipped out 2,000 navvies to New South Wales. Though their fares were paid, they were not obliged to take up work on the railways; Brassey gambled – successfully as it turned out – that they would find little alternative employment, certainly not at the wages he was paying. Return fares were not paid, and Brassey congratulated himself, on dubious grounds, for providing Australia with a desirable class of immigrants.

There were still plenty of railways to be built, but competition was much greater than it had been in the early days, and the big jobs were usually to be found only in countries whose credit was doubtful. But Brassey was not afraid to take a gamble, and his most daring project in these years was a 250-mile railway in Argentina. This line too Brassey himself never saw, but he had a knowledgeable partner who had surveyed the route, and the terms were good: a government guarantee of seven per cent on the total capital subscribed by the company. What could not be guaranteed, of course, was that the government would still be there to pay up. The Central Argentine Railway was constructed more on the American pattern, with hefty excavations avoided as far as possible and low trestle bridges over rivers; in places, the sleepers were laid on the bare earth. As part of the payment, the company was given a strip of land beside the railway in non-built-up areas, which Brassey expected to sell profitably to future settlers. 'The railway will populate the desert,' the Argentine president had forecast, but the anticipated land fever never developed, and although Brassey made a profit, the railway company, operating from London, never managed to work the line as successfully as had been anticipated. Brassey sold his interests in it after a year or two.

From about 1850, the contractors represented one of the chief sources of finance for railway building (Brassey's assets amounted to something like £5 million). Where capital was not otherwise available, the contractor would usually be paid for the construction with shares in the railway, offered at a considerable discount so that he would be able to sell them at a comparable profit in the market. There was one obvious drawback to this system: it worked only in a boom. If there was no demand for shares, as in the case of the Grand Trunk Railway of Canada, the contractor was badly out of pocket, perhaps bankrupt.

Unfortunately, railways were for various reasons rather susceptible to booms and slumps. The early 1860s were a boom period, when in Britain many lines were built that never showed a profit (though most lingered for close on a century). The slump came in 1866 – predictably, it might be said, though at the time it took almost everyone by surprise.

Speculative booms may be followed by collapse inevitably, but there are usually particular reasons for any commercial slump. The trouble in 1866 could be traced to the growth of finance companies in the previous ten years, following the extension of the limited liability law in 1855. These companies tended to deal in shares in large enterprises, such as railways, which did not yet exist. One of the biggest and most respectable was the long-established house of Overend and

Gurney, which had recently embarked on some chancy business. Needing more capital, Overend and Gurney transformed themselves into a limited company, and their good reputation ensured an eager market for the shares; but in fact the position was already hopeless. Unable to produce sound securities for a loan which would have staved off disaster, Overend and Gurney closed their doors with liabilities of £19 million. The result was the crash of the whole fragile edifice of the financial world: there was an immediate and devastating run on the banks; many investors, big and small, were ruined – Sir Morton Peto was among the casualties; the Bank Rate rose to a then sensational ten per cent, and stayed there for three months. Credit became almost unobtainable. Brassey was one of the very few who managed to procure a loan – £30,000. It was enough to cover his wages bill for about ten days!

Brassey's simplest course would have been to cease work everywhere, thus stopping the enormous weekly drain of the wages bill. He was sixty-one, an age at which he might have retired and lived comfortably on the revenue of his property, but Brassey was not the retiring sort. He chose to carry on, hoping that somehow he could complete his current contracts, sinking all he could raise – he even raided a trust fund he had set up for his family – in the effort to carry on.

His salvation came through the Lemberg (Lvov)-Czernowitz (Chernovtsky) Railway, which he was building for the Austrian government. The line was not far from completion, but had been brought to a stop by the outbreak of the Austro-Prussian war. Fortunately for Brassey and his employees, the war lasted only six weeks, though that was long enough for one of Brassey's agents to undertake a hair-raising ride through the battlefield on a commandeered engine with the wages for the workmen, who were on the point of giving up and going home. The railway was finished in September, five months ahead of schedule; bonds to the value of £1 million, which Brassey had accepted in payment, became saleable when the Austrian government's guarantee came into effect on completion of the line, and Brassey thus acquired means to keep his other contracts going until the market improved. He survived, and perhaps of all Brassey's operations, his survival of the crash of 1866 was his greatest achievement.

During the next four years, Brassey built another 550 miles of railway in various countries, mainly in eastern Europe; but his health did not long survive the hectic summer of 1866. He was very ill with bronchitis in 1867, and the following year he suffered a stroke. He made a good recovery and, though one leg remained permanently affected, that did not prevent him visiting work sites and, to the consternation of his friends, crossing a fifty-foot drop along a twelve-inch plank. In 1869, he made another of the whirlwind tours of Europe which had become a feature of his later years, and was greeted in places where he was well known by large crowds, waving flags, and the firing of guns in salute. In England the following year he was still to be seen at the work sites, chatting with many old acquaintances, though by this time he knew he had incurable cancer. In the autumn he withdrew to Hastings where, comforted by his strong religious faith, he endured his last long and painful illness. Many people, old navvies as well as former partners, travelled a great distance to visit him before he died, on December 8 1870. At the time of his death, it has been calculated that of all the railways in the world, approximately one mile in twenty had been built by Thomas Brassey.

4 Iron Roads in the West

A major theme of American history in the nineteenth century was the movement west to occupy the lands beyond the Appalachians. The far west was already quite thickly populated – the total population of Spanish California was larger than that of New York State in 1790 – but connected with the east only by a sea voyage lasting months. The westward movement got under way with the defeat of the French in 1763, but at first it was comparatively slow, due to Indian resistance and the discouragement of the British authorities. The latter ceased to be a factor after 1783, but new problems arose with the conflicting claims of the various states to western territories, problems which were not settled until 1802. The lead in settling new areas was often taken by commercial companies, like John Cleves Symmes's Miami Company, which purchased two million acres of what became known as Cincinnati as a speculation at less than $1 an acre and encouraged settlers to take up residence.

The more distant western settlements were almost completely out of touch with the east. Largely self-sufficient, they could sell only products such as furs which would stand a long and expensive overland journey by wagon. Bulkier goods, such as timber or grain, had to go down the Mississippi, a long and hazardous journey even after the introduction of steamboats on the river.

The westward movement had begun to accelerate early in the nineteenth century. The purchase of Louisiana from Napoleon in 1803 opened up the prospect of expansion beyond the Mississippi, currently inhabited by only a handful of pioneers. Lewis and Clark mapped out a transcontinental route and in 1811 John Jacob Astor established his trading post on the Columbia River, already being visited occasionally by American ships. A trade route from Santa Fe was in regular operation from 1829, and farmers followed traders into California. The south-western states were surrendered by Mexico in 1848, the same year in which the discovery of gold sent the get-rich-quick hopefuls flocking into California, while in the north the long argument over the Oregon territory was settled when the British backed off to the present line of the Canadian border.

The original attitude of the Federal government towards the vast accessions of new territory, which dwarfed the original thirteen states, was that the land should be used for revenue purposes, to reduce taxation and pay off the National Debt; much land was sold to speculators in large lots. From 1820, however, a different policy was adopted, priority being given to providing homes for settlers who would develop the country. Despite opposition in the east, where it was feared that property values would suffer from the easy availability of land in the west, land was sold off in smaller lots and at a low price – $1.25 an acre. The low price of land in the west led to a fantastic land speculation in the 1830s as land values rose; many settlers followed the policy of 'settle and sell' – buying land for settlement, improving it, selling up after a few years at a large profit, and moving farther west to repeat the process. Some indication of the profits to be made in land may be gathered in the – admittedly exceptional – movement of prices in the infant city of Chicago: an acre in Chicago, like other land in the west, could be bought in the 1820s for $1.25 and sold in the mid-1830s for $3,500.

Land in the public domain was also freely disposed of to individuals, institutions or states to encourage internal improvements, such as communications, and between 1840 and 1860 Congress recklessly doled out vast acreages *gratis*. Between those dates, in fact, out of a total of 270 million acres disposed of by Congress, only 69 million were actually sold.

The land filled up ever more quickly. First came the pioneers on the wagon trails – often following the routes of migratory elk and moose – and on river rafts. Then came the farmers, on turnpike roads and canals, and finally came the capitalists, who travelled by railroad – the 'soul of western civilization', as an English visitor described it. The rail-borne capitalists turned log-built villages into permanent, prosperous towns, which were intimately connected with the older settled areas in the east and no longer showed much trace of their frontier origin.

Pioneers with their covered wagons resting on the westward trail

If western expansion is the key to American history in the nineteenth century, then transportation is the key to western expansion. On the far side of the Appalachians there was no easy communication with the east by water; the growth of cities and the concentration of industry depended on improving transportation. On that also depended, less obviously but more importantly, the unity of the country itself. Without efficient communications between the states and territories, the union might well have broken apart. In 1803 Jefferson had said that the country beyond the Mississippi might not be fully settled for a thousand years. Though it

Hazards of road travel: a stage-coach precariously negotiating a mountain track in Virginia

seems a remarkably inaccurate forecast now, he spoke before the days of steamboats and railways, and probably few would have disagreed with him.

Between 1790 and 1815 the roads were much improved by turnpikes, roads built by private companies and financed out of tolls. In the post-Revolutionary era roads were extremely bad – even English visitors commented adversely, and Macadam had not yet gone to work in England. On a journey from Baltimore to Washington in 1795 the roads were said to be so bad that 'a carriage will sometimes sink so deep as to defy the utmost exertions of the strongest horse to draw it forwards; and in some parts that would be otherwise totally impassable, causeways constructed of trees are thrown across the road; but these frequently break asunder and constantly expose a traveler to the most imminent danger. The bridges . . . are equally perilous, being formed of a few loose boards that totter while a carriage passes over them.' The first turnpike road was built between Lancaster and Philadelphia in 1794. It proved successful and so encouraged others: in the next thirty years over 2,000 miles of turnpike were built in Pennsylvania alone. That uniquely American phenomenon, the plank road, was utilized in many places. It would support the heaviest wagon and for farmers was more convenient than a macadamized road. Indeed, in the early days of railroads, many people believed that plank roads offered a preferable alternative, and in Alabama there was a case of a railroad company surrendering to competition from a plank road. Though roads were constructed by private companies, they often received state aid, and in 1808 the Federal government stepped in with a major plan for transportation improvements, the most memorable result of which was the Cumberland Road, to St Louis, completed except for one short stretch by 1838.

Road transport of goods was, however, very expensive. It cost ten times as much per ton to shift freight from Pittsburgh to Philadelphia as it did to ship it from Philadelphia to London. Virtually all bulk goods therefore went by water. The Mississippi was the major route for western traffic: grain, flour, cotton, etc., floated freely down it on flat boats, but it was more of a problem getting goods upstream. Poling keelboats against the current was a prodigious labour, requiring the legendary strength of a Mike Fink.

The navigable waterways came into their own with the development of the steamboat. Experiments with steamers went well back into the eighteenth century, but they did not become a practical proposition until Robert Fulton's *Clermont* chugged from New York to Albany and back on the Hudson in 1807. The *New Orleans* descended the Ohio and the Mississippi in 1812 but could not make the return journey. Four years later, the *Enterprise* successfully battled the current all the way to Louisville, which she reached twenty-five days after leaving New Orleans, and inaugurated regular steamboat traffic on the Mississippi. Expansion was rapid. In the year that Robert Fulton confounded a nearly universally sceptical public with his trip to Albany, the value of goods reaching New Orleans was $5 million; by 1860 it was $185 million (over half of it cotton). At that date there were over one thousand steamers on the Mississippi and its tributaries, while the effect of steamboat traffic on the Great Lakes had turned places such as Cleveland and Detroit from villages of one or two thousand people in 1830 to cities of about 45,000 inhabitants.

The great era of the steamboats in the United States, like the era of the speedy mail coach in England, was glorious but short. 'Mississippi steamboating was born about 1812,' wrote Mark Twain; 'at the end of thirty years it had grown to

Robert Fulton's side-paddle steamboat, the Clermont, *advancing triumphantly against the current in the Hudson River. This appears to be an enlarged version of the original boat, which remained in service until 1914*

mighty proportions; and in less than thirty more it was dead! A strangely short life for so majestic a creature.'

Steamboats or not, large areas of the growing country, such as western New York State and northern Ohio, were virtually bereft of water transport because they lacked navigable rivers. The answer here, as in England, was canals. New York State began the digging of the Erie Canal in 1817 (it had first been mooted at least twenty-five years earlier; moreover, in 1812 John Stevens of Hoboken, New Jersey, had suggested that a railway would be better than a canal). In the remarkably short time of eight years the connection between the Hudson River and Lake Erie was successfully completed. The cost of construction was $7 million, but it was recouped from tolls within nine years. However the success of the enterprise was more visibly evident in the prosperity of towns such as Rochester, Utica and Buffalo, which by 1838 were receiving more grain for trans-shipment than New Orleans. The Erie Canal made New York the largest American port, out-stripping Philadelphia; freight charges between Buffalo and New York were reduced from $100 a ton to just $5, and time in transit from twenty days to six.

The Erie Canal created for the first time a close economic bond between the east and the west, and its effects on economic development generally would be hard to exaggerate. Its success led to something of a 'canal mania' similar to the one that

followed the building of the Bridgewater Canal in England: by
1840 Pennsylvania had more than a thousand miles of man-
made waterway. The most important were those in the west
which linked Lake Erie with the Ohio, to the great advantage of
the farmers of northern Ohio; but none was quite as successful as
the Erie.

Constitutional objections had checked the work of the
Federal government in direct subsidizing of internal improvements, which inevitably benefited certain regions and not
others. But private capital proved insufficient to finance the
big projects in communications and transportation, including
railroads, that were under way in the 1830s; state aid was
required, the states being better able than private corporations
to raise large loans. In this boom period, state legislatures, led on
by the availability of easy money, by the desire not to fall behind
their neighbours in the race for internal improvements, and by
the general feverish speculative atmosphere, threw money

*The Erie Canal at
Buffalo, N.Y., in 1885,
by which time it was
looking a little seedy. In
the 1830s the Canal
opened the whole Great
Lakes area, vastly
facilitated westward
immigration and, unlike
the many subsidiaries it
spawned, operated at a
profit*

about in a manner that was over-ambitious to say the least. A great deal of it was borrowed from England, where capital was plentiful and interest rates comparatively low.

The boom collapsed in the great panic of 1837. Wise men saw the crash coming: in 1836 only 175 miles of railroads were built compared with 465 in 1835, while the vast investments in land were proving less profitable than sanguine investors had expected. Money tightened up, cotton prices fell and a number of English banks most closely involved in American cotton were forced to close. The crash revealed that many enterprises were at best unnecessary as well as unprofitable, many were badly or corruptly managed, and, in general, much cash had been foolishly squandered. Several states repudiated their debts, to the immense irritation of their English creditors; Sydney Smith declared that he could not sit down to dinner with a citizen of Pennsylvania (one of the defaulters) 'without feeling a disposition to seize and divide him – to allot his beaver to one sufferer and his coat to another – to appropriate his pocket handkerchief to the orphan, and to comfort the widow with his silver watch. . . .' However, most state debts were eventually honoured, at least in part.

One general effect of the panic was that states tended to withdraw from active involvement in the construction of new communication links, selling off existing works to private buyers. Some states actually passed amendments to their constitutions expressly forbidding the employment of state funds in internal improvements. Thus, at the beginning of the Railway Age, both Federal and state governments were restricted from direct participation in systems of communication and transportation. The job fell to private enterprise – more specifically to corporations, which now began their unparalleled progress to vast economic and political power.

The precise origins of railways in the United States are as hard to pin down as they are in England, but it is usually agreed that the first public railway, corresponding to the Stockton and Darlington in England, was the Baltimore and Ohio Railroad, part of which opened in 1830. It had wooden rails with an iron strip laid along the top; this had an unfortunate habit of snapping upwards under the pressure of the wheels and penetrating the floors of the carriages, which

The Baltimore and Ohio Railroad in 1832, with carriages made from obsolescent stage-coaches

were converted stage-coaches. Although the railroad soon made use of locomotives, at first it employed horses and even experimented with sails. Other early railways were mostly short city lines, more like tramways than railroads as we think of them today, although in South Carolina the Charleston and Hamburg, 137 miles in length, was the longest line in the world under one management when it opened in 1833. By comparison with what was to come, progress was slow throughout the 1830s and 1840s, partly due to the depression which set in after the panic of 1837 and persisted into the late 1840s. Thereafter, progress accelerated remarkably. The total mileage of railroads open in 1850 was more than trebled during the ensuing decade, when more miles of railroad were laid in the United States than in the whole of Europe.

The first locomotives were imported from England, but they proved too heavy for the American track and encouraged some sceptics in the belief that steam locomotion would never work. The problems were overcome quite soon by American engineers. One of the first successful American steam locomotives was Peter Cooper's *Tom Thumb*, whose performance on the Baltimore and Ohio Railroad in 1831 convinced the proprietors that the mobile steam engine was the right answer; cast-iron rails, on the other hand, did not come into general use until the mid-1840s.

Two early steam locomotives. Peter Cooper's Tom Thumb, top, *easily outstrips its horse-drawn rival on the Baltimore and Ohio line in 1830, and the De Witt Clinton,* below, *the first steam locomotive in New York state, makes its first trip in 1831 on the Mohawk and Hudson line*

Another problem delaying the development of large railroad systems was the difference in gauges, which necessitated frequent shifting of goods from one track to the next at junctions. There was no general agreement on a standard gauge until the 1850s, and even then it was not universally adopted. After the Civil War, standardization became widespread, though the Erie Railroad kept its six-foot gauge until 1878 and a few lines were not standardized until the end of the century.

A few early railroads were built by private individuals, though far more were constructed by corporations. Capital was not easy to raise. There was a great deal of ignorance and popular resistance. A politician in Indiana irritated the voters by suggesting it was possible to travel on a railroad at thirty miles an hour; any fool knew that a human being would not survive at such a speed. Rather more significant was opposition from various vested interests, including the proprietors of stage-coach lines and canals. State governments were often sensitive to these interests. A railroad company in New York was compelled to buy out a competing turnpike company at a generous price as a condition of its charter. New York was even more nervous about the effects of competition on its particular brainchild, the Erie Canal, going so far as to legislate a ban on the carriage of freight by railroads except in the winter months when the canal was not in use, though in 1851, when the full potential of railroads was becoming evident, the ban was rescinded.

Originally, though, railroads were seen in the east mainly as feeders for waterways; not for several years did they develop into rivals. Even then, water transport was generally much cheaper, certainly for bulk goods such as timber or grain, and in the latter case it could also be argued that, from the farmers' point of view, the slow transit time was an advantage, as it militated against post-harvest gluts. Apart from the cost factor, and the more dubious one of avoiding glutted markets, the railroads had the advantage. Unlike waterways, they were not subject to the limitations of topography: the distance between Cincinnati and St Louis was 720 miles by water but only 327 by rail. Nor were their operations interrupted by climate: in the north, nearly all water-borne traffic came to a standstill in the freezing winter months (a problem that English, or southern, canals did not have to contend with), while the trains puffed cheerfully onward. It has been argued that this consistency of service was the railroad's most weighty virtue. Finally, the railroads were much faster, and whatever the farmers – or more likely the canal owners – might say, speed in transit is generally a great commercial advantage. By 1860, about two-thirds of US internal trade was carried by railroads.

In spite of the general withdrawal of governments from expenditure on internal improvements, the railroads could hardly have been built without state aid, direct or indirect. Railroads benefited more than other industries in the generation before the Civil War, partly because in an age when agrarian interests were politically dominant, railroads offered substantial advantages to farmers. Probably the most important form of Federal government assistance they received was through land grants. Land grants had been made earlier to assist in the construction of roads and canals, where their importance was more than a purely local one, and in the 1850s this form of subsidy was adopted for railroads. Blocks of land six miles square in a zig zag line were made available to the State of Illinois, which passed them on to the Illinois Central Railroad in exchange for seven per cent of the gross earnings of the railroad, when it came into operation. The grant gained Congressional approval through the improved connections which the railroad would create with the Atlantic states (gaining eastern votes) and a similar grant made to the projected Mobile and Ohio Railroad, which attracted southern votes. By 1860, land grants to railroads totalled over 30 million acres, and after the Civil War they became still more lavish.

In their eagerness to get their own towns and cities on a future railroad, local legislators were prepared to grant almost any privilege to railroad companies, such as monopoly of traffic on a given route. The states also helped by taking up stock, guaranteeing railroad securities, and by loans: Ohio authorized a loan of credit amounting to one-third of the railroad company's capital, while between 1850 and 1857 the states of Minnesota and Missouri used their credit to buy railroad bonds amounting to a total of over $20 million. Railroad companies were permitted to finance costs of construction by the issue of banknotes whose only security was the railroad – a railroad not yet built.

These methods certainly encouraged railroad building, but no less certainly they prevented orderly planning and development and encouraged extravagance and speculation. Some railroads were promoted with the sole object of securing land grants for funding railroad banks, and were therefore built as cheaply as possible, then sold off at the first opportunity or allowed to fold. In Mississippi between 1831 and the panic of 1837, wrote Cleveland and Powell, the state was 'gridironed with imaginary railroads, and beridden with railroad banks. In these enterprises there was more watered stock sold than cross-ties laid; reckless speculation brooked nothing as prosaic as the actual construction of railroads, on the successful operation of which it was supposed fabulous dividends would be declared.'

There is nearly always an important divergence of aims between industry and business. The business of industry is efficient production of goods or, in the case of railroads, of transportation, while the business of business is profit; the two aims are seldom identical and may well be in conflict. Even the alliance between George Stephenson and George Hudson, very close in the early years of Hudson's career, became tenuous after Hudson's operations in connection with the Newcastle and Darlington Junction Railway, of which Stephenson disapproved, and in the United States the difference between the aims of the railroad engineer and the railroad financier were often more obviously at variance. The railroad engineer, as an engineer (some, of course, had additional interests), was merely concerned with building a technically efficient railroad; the financier was concerned with making the maximum profit out of the work, which might include economizing on materials and overcharging on construction, as in the Crédit Mobilier scandal. Thus a Vanderbilt or a Daniel Drew was a great railroad man not so much because of the improvements he initiated in transport but rather because he was adept at manipulating railroad securities.

Because of the huge amounts of capital required, railroads could, with a few exceptions, be built only by corporations. The stock, or shares, of the corporation were held increasingly by a large and diverse group, including the famous widow with her humble savings, and the directors were in the happy position of controlling large quantities of money which they could employ more or less as they wished, with little risk to themselves. As in England during the railway mania of the 1840s, the stockholders – the actual owners of the corporation – had little or no say in what happened to the money. It was impossible to wield the stockholders into a single unit, and attempts to exert some control over the company's affairs could usually be easily thwarted by the power of the directors, armed with proxies. At a stockholders' meeting of the Erie Railroad in 1854, the stockholders put up a list of their own nominees for the Board, but their list was easily defeated by the

*The New York Stock
Exchange in 1885*

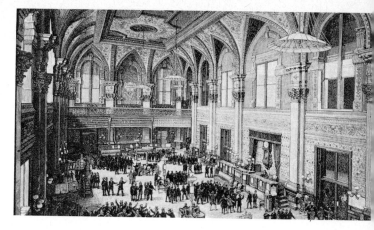

incumbent directors, who held a large number of proxies and had managed to prevent publication of the report of a recent inquiry into the company's affairs, which had reached a highly adverse verdict on their conduct.

Railroads had greater success than other industries in getting what they wanted from government because they could command wider support. The fiercest battles in Congress and the state legislatures over railroad bills were frequently waged not by the supporters and opponents of railroads but by rival railroad companies. Railroad lobbyists were immensely powerful; they had vast amounts of money available and few moral scruples to prevent their using it for more or less corrupt purposes. Straightforward cash bribery was often unnecessary, though legislators were freely offered railroad stock, or free travel facilities, or merely stock-market tips which enabled them to net a handsome sum by foreknowledge of railroad companies' plans. But besides bribery of this kind, the legislators were often open to railroad pressure because of their desire to ensure that their own town or district was not left in the unrailroaded wasteland; a goodly number of votes in state legislatures could often be secured merely by promising that the railroad would pass through particular places. Moreover, the whole social atmosphere worked to the advantage of the railroad companies. Railroads were universally seen as the harbingers of civilization, as well as merely the makers of profits, so that it was not difficult for the ordinary representative to convince himself that even if the methods of the railroad companies (and these methods were not, of course, confined to the railroad industry) were corrupt or illegal, they were in a good cause.

The biggest scandals came to light in the post-war era, but there were some startling revelations in the earlier period. In 1856, for example, the La Crosse and Milwaukee Railroad Company won a million acres of land in Wisconsin through the expenditure of $900,000 in securities to Assemblymen, State Senators and officials of the state government. The Governor's private secretary received $5,000, while the Governor himself got ten times as much. He was wise enough to sell quickly. Though he received only about one-third of face value for his bonds, those who held on to them received nothing at all, for the railroad company went bankrupt in the wake of the slump of 1857. There were other, similar affairs (and no doubt some that have never emerged into the light of day), enough to show that the extravagant corruption and fraud associated with the 'gilded age' after the Civil War was well established before 1861.

Between 1850 and 1857 the capitalists of the north-east grew richer and more powerful thanks to the rapid industrial development which they financed. As it became annually more evident, the economic domination of the north was regarded with increasing resentment in the south. Then with the election of Lincoln in 1860, political power as well was at last wrested from the old planter aristocracy of the south. The south was defeated by an alliance of northern capitalists and western farmers, for in recent years the interests of the latter had become more closely linked with the north than the south. 'It is scarcely too much to say', wrote Fred A. Shannon, 'that the West was held loyal ... by the existence of through connections to Eastern ports.' Faced with political defeat on top of economic domination, the south decided on secession, and the Civil War became inevitable. In due course the victory of the Union merely confirmed the fear of the south that its power had gone for good, while the Republican Party in the post-war era emerged as pre-eminently the party of 'big business', the western interests from which it had largely sprung having become strictly subordinate.

Business was depressed in 1860 in the wake of the slump of 1857, and the imminence of war depressed it further. War, however, is generally inflationary, and the Civil War soon

Railways were both the cause and result of industrial development generally. The steel industry, in particular, benefitted from the enormous demand for steel rails, which convinced Andrew Carnegie of the wisdom of turning over to steel in the 1870s

stimulated production and turned slump into boom. Though some railroads, especially in the south, were ruined, others that had hitherto made no profit returned large dividends in 1863–64 thanks to greatly increased traffic; western railroads profited from the closure of the Mississippi. Many disreputable suppliers made vast fortunes from sales of more or less shoddy provisions and war supplies. In the first year of the war, Union soldiers wore uniforms imported from abroad; in the last year of the war the United States was an exporter of field artillery. Congress kept manufacturers happy with high tariffs, with an act exempting immigrant workers from military service, and other laws. It acted – apparently – to keep the west happy with the Homestead Act, which granted plots of 160 acres in the public domain to anyone who would cultivate them for five years, with an option to purchase within six months at $1.25 an acre. But the effect of this latter provision was to encourage land speculation on a massive scale. It was not difficult to install phoney settlers who promptly exercised their option to purchase, whereupon the land could be resold to genuine settlers at a dizzy profit: by 1870 former public-domain land in Kansas was selling for $15 an acre.

A similar tendency to favour northern business rather than western agrarian interests was apparent in the treatment of transcontinental railroads which, long mooted, and currently appearing as a strategic necessity, were chartered during the Civil War – sharply stimulating land speculation. The projected railroads received, besides many millions in government bonds, a total of 70 million acres in the public domain. By its very nature this land was especially valuable because of the promised proximity of transportation facilities. (Land grants were conditional on the line in question actually being constructed, so the total eventually received by the railroad companies was rather less than the total authorized.) Senator Howe of Wisconsin complained that railroad grants were turning the west into 'little more than a province of New York', while the Emigrant Aid Company was soon to be found pursuing a precisely opposite purpose from that for which its title suggested it existed. Far from encouraging settlers in the west, its publicity emphasized the difficulties confronting them, the company being far more interested in selling the lands.

The victory of the Republicans and the need to organize for war led to a rapid advance in the power of the Federal government *vis-à-vis* the states; railroad companies and others looked increasingly to Washington. The Union Pacific was the first railroad company to receive a Federal charter (1862), and the first to receive land grants direct from the Federal government. In 1864 its charter was revised in order

Railways played a vital role in the Civil War, in spite of mishaps like the derailing of a train carrying reinforcements for the Confederate General Johnston in darkest Mississippi in 1862

to increase both its capital and its land grant, which was doubled. The company's lobbyists in Washington spent nearly $500,000 in gaining these advantages, while several Congressmen became directly involved with the Crédit Mobilier, the construction company which existed not so much to build the Pacific railroad as to make illicit profits for its proprietors. It was set up by the directors of the Union Pacific and received altogether about $75 million, subscribed by government and by private investors, to cover the costs of construction. The true costs, however, were not more than $50 million, which left a tidy surplus for the directors' personal appropriation. A very similar swindle was operated by the Central Pacific (which was built westward to meet the Union Pacific advancing from the east). The contributions of Congress alone to the first transcontinental railroad exceeded the total cost of its construction, but Congress saw no return for many years as the profit of the railroad went not to repaying government loans but to other purposes such as the building of branch lines and, in one way or another, into the proprietors' pockets. The half-dozen leading members of the Central Pacific all left over $40 million when they died.

The originally scheduled meeting point for the Union Pacific and the Central Pacific in the Far West was abandoned during construction and the two companies raced to make the greatest number of miles of track in order to secure the largest land grants. There was no bonus for straightness, so the easiest route was followed: embankments and cuttings, being too expensive and time-consuming, were avoided as far as possible (though a good deal of tunnelling was required on the Central Pacific's sections). In spite of the fact that at times half the workforce was employed in fighting the Indians work proceeded at astonishing speed: the Union Pacific averaged over two miles a day for a long period, and on one memorable day laid eight miles between dawn and sunset. The speed was less astonishing, perhaps, when the actual methods of construction were taken into account. Over long stretches, the Irish labourers of the Union Pacific (the Central Pacific used gangs of Chinese) merely flung down the ties, or sleepers, and spiked the rails on top, not even bothering to ensure that each rail joint was supported by a crosstie. It was hardly surprising that the track of the Union Pacific, as of other

land-grant railroads, had to be replaced after a very short period in use. This, it has often been said, is the most serious charge against the railroad magnates – not that they watered stock and creamed off capital but that they built poor railroads.

The rapid industrial expansion which began in the later years of the Civil War depended largely on mechanization and capital. In other words, it was the big manufacturers who expanded; others, who could not raise the necessary capital, were bought up, or went out of business. Millionaires became common: 'the power accumulating in the moneyed classes from the concentration of capital in large masses is attracting the attention of the close observers of the money market,' remarked one of the latter. 'It is one of the signs of the time and will probably exert no small influence over the future growth of our industrial and commercial enterprise.' After the Civil War, 'big business' ruled, and the law of 'big business' was the law of the jungle. Corporations, identified as 'persons' by the Supreme Court in its interpretation of the Fourteenth Amendment which denied the states power to deprive persons of property without due process of law, became 'super-persons, as incorporeal as angels and as little amenable to punishment, in mysterious ways directing the life of the new society, but seemingly outside its laws'.[5] The leaders in the race for progress and profit were the railroad men. Between 1865 and 1893, 150,000 miles of track were opened and railroad

American railway builders specialized in lightweight construction which made up in cheapness what it lacked in durability. This type of truss bridge was patented by Squire Whipple of Rensselaer County, N.Y., in 1847

125

capital reached nearly $10 billion. Railroad men employed their vast resources without care or scruple. The Central Pacific in the 1870s spent $500,000 in obtaining loans and subsidies, fighting competition and on capturing the public domain for private gain. Senator Howe's complaint seemed justified by the revelation that, in some western states, as much as one-quarter of the total area had been granted to railroad companies. The County of Los Angeles contributed $600,000, equivalent to $100 a head of its population, to the Southern Pacific, and similar grants were made by other local governments, frequently to railroad companies which never got around to laying any track. Federal land grants to railroad companies between 1862 and 1872 totalled 200 million acres (nearly half of which never actually came into the companies' possession due to uncompleted construction) and Federal loans in the same period approached $65 million. Some counties and cities incurred debts as a result of railroad grants in the 1870s which they were still paying off in the next century.

Railroad promoters were able to use their various grants from the Federal and local governments as guarantees for private loans, but despite that advantage, it was still often difficult to raise the required capital. Whatever their long-term potential, railroads were inevitably slow to return a profit, especially when they were built in areas where as yet little or no traffic existed. Private investors at home and abroad found other alternatives more attractive, and railroad companies therefore frequently sold their stock below par, which led to overcapitalization and consequent high prices in order to pay interest on debts. Once the initial difficulties of raising capital were overcome, railroad promoters looked to make their fortunes not out of the working of the railroad, usually a relatively distant prospect, but by more or less dubious manipulation of its stock and by appropriation of capital, as in the Crédit Mobilier affair. The classic case of an unprofitable railroad being employed as a means of creating private fortunes is that of the Erie in the hands of Daniel Drew, Jay Gould and Jim Fisk. Naturally, not all railroad men were rogues like these; a man like J. Edgar Thomson, architect of the Pennsylvania Railroad system, was never interested in stock manipulation, merely in building a great and prosperous railway, while James J. Hill showed that what made a railway profitable was the business of carrying people and goods.

Nevertheless, doubtful and dishonest practices were widespread. In defence of the railroad magnates, it can be argued that the American railroad system, especially in the west, could hardly have been built by other methods. In those times no enterprise could be entertained which did not offer profits, and as there was no chance of a railroad earning a profit in the immediate future (construction of the transcontinental railroads averaged about twelve years), the profit had to come from capital.

Even railroads that were highly profitable often found their profits jeopardized by the pressure of competition. The artificial stimulus of land grants added to other economic incentives had led to serious over-construction. In older countries railroads joined centres of population; in the United States they were often built, like the Union Pacific, ahead of any settled population and had to struggle desperately to attract traffic. Once a railroad is in operation, its costs are more or less fixed, regardless of the quantity of business: it costs little more to run a full train than an empty one. In the prevailing atmosphere of rampant individualism, heightened by the belief in that twisted modification of evolutionary theory enunciated in Herbert Spencer's famous phrase, 'survival of the fittest', railroad companies indulged in cut-throat competition in efforts to filch each other's traffic, in which nothing – not even violence on occasion – was barred.

One fairly typical abuse was discrimination in charges. Where there was no competition, rates were extremely high, sometimes high enough to make it unprofitable for farmers to ship their produce to market, and having to burn corn as fuel because it was too expensive to move it did not make farmers warm admirers of the railroad. Agrarian resentment lent strength to the Granger movement, a kind of pastoral masonic order whose considerable energies in the early 1870s were diverted into a political war against 'railroad pirates' and 'Wall-Street stock-jobbers'; several states passed 'Granger laws' for controlling and regulating railroad charges, but they were mostly repealed after a few years as a result of the railroad companies' determined publicity campaigns and their powerful influence among legislators. Where com-

The Granger movement as seen by Thomas Nast, with a farmer and a businessman eyeing each other suspiciously

petition did exist, rates were slashed to absurdly uneconomic levels, the loss being made good on the expensive, non-competitive routes. It cost $3.25 to ship a bale of cotton the 275 miles from Minona, Mississippi, where there was no competition, to New Orleans in the 1880s. To ship the same bale from Memphis, where competition was fierce, cost only $1, although the distance involved was far greater. Special rates were granted to certain companies in order to secure a monopoly of their custom, while the cost of that was recouped from less important shippers whose business was less vital. 'Railway officials', as Andrew Carnegie wrote, 'could make or unmake mining and manufacturing concerns.' To overcome legal objections, the big shippers were often charged at the fixed rate but received a rebate later, 'perhaps the most vicious abuse', wrote John Moody, 'of which the railroads have ever been guilty.' Nonetheless, this practice continued until specifically forbidden by law in 1887.

One answer to competition was amalgamation. Some amalgamations had been carried out since the 1850s, mostly of consecutive short lines to form a single trunk line. The strong popular suspicion of monopolies prevented some amalgamations taking place, but there was a contrary pressure in favour of better co-ordination of railroad services which allowed other amalgamations to come into effect. The first trunk line from Chicago to the Atlantic coast was one early result. Under men like Cornelius Vanderbilt, great railroad systems were created and many small companies absorbed, but whatever advantages the new empires had, they did not end competition. Although the number of competitors was fewer, the war between rival empires was even more intense, and the result was a series of savage rate wars. One prime example took place on the route between New York and Chicago in the 1870s in which first-class freight rates were slashed from $18.80 a hundredweight to just $1.50.

Some attempts were made to eliminate ruinous competition by the formation of pools, in which competing companies made an agreement to standardize rates and put a proportion of their profits into a common pool, to be divided equally among them. Some pools worked fairly well, for a time at least, but their fatal weakness was that they had no legal standing. They depended on a gentlemen's agreement, and a line that was doing badly was always likely to surrender to the temptation to break the agreement by reducing charges. As James J. Hill, himself a great rate-cutter, put it, 'a starving railway will not maintain rates'. The general tendency was towards monopoly – the formation of the railroads in a particular area into one giant combination headed by a Hill or a Harriman – in spite of frequent popular protests and numerous attempts to exert some form of government control.

The creation of the Interstate Commerce Commission by the act of 1887 was one attempt to prevent such abuses as discriminatory or unreasonable rates. But the ICC proved a paper tiger. It could only enforce its decisions through the courts, and while a given case made its ponderous way ever upwards through the various tribunals involved, the accused railroad company happily continued its alleged malpractices. When the matter finally came before the Supreme Court, the justices in the vast majority of cases found in favour of the railroad company. The Sherman Anti-Trust Act of 1890 would, if strictly interpreted, have made almost any form of combination illegal, but the Supreme Court again took a conservative view and lawyers found the act easy to penetrate: 'What looks like a stone-wall to a layman is a triumphal arch to a corporation lawyer,' said Mr Dooley, and 'big business' eventually came to smile kindly on the Sherman Act when it

The meeting of the Union Pacific and the Central Pacific in Utah on May 10, 1869, completing the first transcontinental rail link

transpired that the type of combination it could be most effectively used against was organized labour. However, both the ICC and the Sherman Act did make life more difficult for the big railroad combinations, and they were important steps on the way to better control of railroads in the public interest.

5 Bandits in the Palace: Gould, Fisk and the Erie

The success of the Erie Canal after its opening in 1825 encouraged demands for a similar transportation route to link the southern counties of New York State with the Great Lakes, and in response to this pressure the New York and Erie Railroad Company was chartered by the New York Legislature in 1832 to supply this need. From the word go, however, the Erie Railroad was beset by problems. Because of difficulties in raising capital, actual construction did not begin until 1836, and in the following year the financial panic brought it temporarily to a halt. The original cost was estimated to be $3 million, but this figure soon proved to be wildly optimistic. The state came to the rescue with a loan of $3 million, but by 1842, when the estimate had risen to $12½ million, the company was bankrupt. The state again stepped in, and agreed to write off the earlier loan, which made it possible for more money to be raised from private subscribers; the section already completed was mortgaged for another $3 million.

The line finally opened in 1851. Using a six-foot gauge, it ran from Piermont on the Hudson, about twenty miles north of New York City, to Dunkirk on Lake Erie, with numerous branches. In spite of the chequered history of its construction, it was a splendid achievement. 'This great route', said a travel brochure of 1857, 'claims a special admiration for the

Daniel Drew

grandeur of the enterprise which conceived and executed it, for the vast contribution it has made to the facilities of travel, and for the multiplied and various landscape beauties which it has made so readily and pleasantly accessible.' However, its capital liabilities in 1851 amounted to $26 million, a disturbing sum compared with the original estimate, or even with the highest estimate of the intervening years, of $15 million. Its charges were accordingly high, and its service proved to be notoriously unreliable, with many accidents, and while it continued to expand, acquiring a number of minor tributaries, it was still dogged with the problems associated with its construction. In 1859 the final blow to the original company fell, when it was unable to pay the interest due on its mortgages and the Erie went into receivership. However, it was thoroughly reorganized in 1861 and its future then looked rosy, since its annual revenue was no less than $16 million.

From the early days of the Erie, the leading power on the board, and for much of the time the company treasurer, was Daniel Drew, and it was Drew who was responsible in the first place for making the Erie not so much a railroad company as a Stock Exchange football – the 'scarlet woman of Wall Street' – whose stock was bought and sold by speculators looking for a quick killing. By his manipulation of Erie stock over the years Drew made himself a very rich man and gained the nickname of the 'speculative director'.

Drew had been born in Putnam County the year after Washington retired from the presidency of the young republic. As a youth, he had driven cattle from his home to the New York market, and it was said that he had devised a trick to make his cattle drink as much water as possible just before the sale to increase their weight. Later, he was to find more profitable ways of 'watering stock'. For some years he was proprietor of the Bull's Head, a tavern on what was then the edge of the city, at 26th Street and Third Avenue. In 1834 he bought his first steamboat and, like his great rival Vanderbilt, it was in steamboats that he made his fortune and laid the foundations for his future career as financier.

Drew never had much education. It was said that 'Uncle Dan'l' could not read too well, and would ask someone else to read a contract to him as he had 'forgotten his eyeglasses'. Whether or not he was guilty of such dissembling, in other respects he was not ashamed of his humble background; he talked like a cattle drover all his days. Shrewd and unscrupulous, he cultivated an appearance of sombre piety, looking, despite his stove-pipe hat, like a Puritan elder oppressed by the thought of Original Sin. Nor was this a mere façade. He did endow a theological college in New Jersey, he disliked being prevented from regular attendance at church, while in business his general outlook was scarcely more hopeful than Jeremiah's estimate of the prospects of his contemporaries. In Stock Market terms he was a natural 'bear', just as Vanderbilt was a natural 'bull' (a 'bear' speculates on the assumption of falling stock prices, a 'bull' on the expectation that prices will rise).

In 1866 'Uncle Dan'l' brought off his most remarkable operation yet in manipulating Erie stock. As usual, the company was short of cash, and as he had frequently done before, the treasurer agreed to make a loan. The sum was $3.5 million, and, as security, he took a large quantity of unissued stock together with $3 million in convertible bonds – bonds which, at the holder's request, could be converted into stock at some future time.

The market was buoyant, Erie stock was scarce, and the price began to rise. Speculators thought they saw an opportunity to make quick profits. Drew was selling, and he was apparently selling 'short' – that is, accepting contracts to sell stock which he did not have. As the price continued to increase and Drew continued to sell, the lines on his face grew deeper; the woes of the world seemed to weigh heavily upon him. It looked as though 'Uncle Dan'l' was cornered.

At the critical moment, with Erie stock approaching par (100), Drew dropped his bomb. His bearish claws seized the collateral on his Erie loan and, having converted the bonds into stock, he suddenly flooded the market with some 58,000 Erie shares. While the bulls bellowed in pain, the price dropped by half. But Uncle Dan'l had sold at around 95, and pocketed about $3 million.

The workings of the stock market are mysterious and bewildering to the layman. The buying and selling frequently bears little obvious relationship to the actual production of goods or provision of services. Stock Exchange operations are a form of gambling, no different in principle from gambling with

Cornelius Vanderbilt

cards or dice, in which, as C. F. Adams put it, 'One man agrees to deliver, at some future time, property which he has not got, to another man who does not care to own it.' The morality of an operation such as Drew's may be compared with the morality of a racehorse owner who dopes a horse to win a race. But in the social atmosphere of the 1860s such operations were generally regarded with more admiration than disapproval. Aha! You had to get up early to put one across 'Uncle Dan'l'. He was a downy bird all right!

Extraordinary though it seemed at the time, Drew's 1866 manipulation was soon to be overshadowed by more astonishing events connected with the Erie Railroad. Already looming up was the great battle for control of the Erie which in 1868 'convulsed the money market, occupied the courts, agitated legislatures, and perplexed the country'. Not the least remarkable feature of this mighty contest was that the opposing commanders, ferocious and formidable sons of Mars, were both in their seventies. In the left corner stood Daniel Drew and in the right, Cornelius Vanderbilt.

Like Drew, Vanderbilt came from a poor family and made his fortune in steamboat lines. He did not much like railroads, but by 1860 he was one of the few who recognized that railroad lines led towards a golden future. He sold his steamboat interests and became a railroad man. Vanderbilt was a bigger man than Drew. Though no less unscrupulous, he did not regard his railroad companies solely as means of making money through stock manipulation. He was a man of grander vision, and his vision encompassed the view that railroad companies were likely to be ruined by savage competition. Equally, he foresaw that the way to prevent it was by buying up rival companies. In short, Vanderbilt was the first to attempt to create a monopolistic railroad empire. Needless to say, it was to be *his* empire, and in 1865, at the age of seventy-one, he began to create it.

The great rival of the Erie Railroad was the New York Central, which also spanned New York State from east to west. The New York Central depended for its entrance to New York City on two small independent lines, the Harlem Railroad and the Hudson River Railroad. Vanderbilt's first step was to obtain control of these lines. About 1862 he began buying Harlem RR stock, which was deep in the doldrums at under

$30 a $100 share. By stock manipulation, Vanderbilt raised the price, and in August 1863, when he brought off a corner, it soared to 179. He made a fortune in the process (it was rumoured that Drew was among the losers), and the following year he repeated the process, when the stock rose dizzily to 285. The Hudson River RR proved almost equally lucrative. Vanderbilt gained control by buying stock at par and soon sent it up to 180. In two or three years he had gained for himself a huge fortune, control of the two railroads, and a reputation to tremble at in the railroad business. He was approached by the managers of the New York Central, eager to benefit from his magic touch, and by 1867 he was in control of that company as well.

Whether Vanderbilt had started out with the idea of establishing his control over the whole railroad system – and thus the trade – of New York, such a monopoly was now clearly possible. It remained only to gain control of the Erie. The real battle now began.

Owing to the way its stock was bartered to and fro, the Erie ownership was always theoretically up for grabs; it was Drew's usual policy, other things being equal, to buy stock when the annual election of directors was approaching and to sell afterwards, when his power had been confirmed. Vanderbilt, with his vast resources, entered the competition in 1867, but matters were complicated by the intervention of a third group. This was made up partly of Boston men who were interested in getting their hands on a money-making machine like the Erie in the interests of a notorious, totally bankrupt outfit called the Boston, Hartford and Erie Railroad, which they owned (the state of Massachusetts had promised a subsidy if a substantial amount of capital could be raised from other sources, and the Erie appeared a likely victim).

It appeared that the battle would be quickly over, for the Vanderbilt group and the Boston group formed an alliance which together seemed able to control enough votes to defeat Drew and his associates. However, Drew was still dangerous, and when he proposed a compromise, Vanderbilt accepted. They agreed that Drew should be dropped from the Board at election time, but that one of the members should afterwards resign, whereupon Drew would be appointed in his place. The Boston group was none too happy with this apparent double-cross, but they soon felt better when they were awarded a slice of the apple in the shape of an Erie guarantee of the interest on $4 million in bonds of the Boston, Hartford and Erie RR. Thus everyone was satisfied except, of course, the ignorant 'outsiders' among the Erie shareholders.

Another aspect of the agreement was the setting up of a 'bull' pool, with Drew as manager, to buy $9 million of Erie stock. Sure enough, the stock soon began to rise, but it did not rise as fast or as far as many had hoped. One member of the pool, Richard Schell, came complaining to Drew about it. Drew's reassurances proved so satisfactory that Schell decided to buy more Erie stock on his own account, while the former agreed to lend him money from the pool to buy it with. However, Erie stock still failed to rise as much as Schell felt it should. He then discovered that the stock he was buying came from a firm of brokers associated with Drew. This was distinctly worrying. At length he came to Drew again, and suggested that, in order to give Erie stock an upward boost, the pool should buy some more. Drew then calmly informed him that the pool owned no Erie stock and certainly had no intention of buying any. It had owned some, but had sold out a short time before at a handsome profit; the proceeds were about to be divided among the members. Schell's reaction may be imagined. Himself a member of the pool, he had unknowingly been buying the pool's own stock – and with money borrowed from the pool! It was but small compensation that his operations as a private buyer had contributed to the profits of the pool of which he was, as a member, entitled to his share.

This little lesson in the dangers and rewards of speculation, however, has nothing directly to do with the great Erie battle, which was soon resumed.

Vanderbilt had improved his position, but he had not yet got control of the Erie. When his proposal that the company should join in an amicable combination with the New York Central and the Pennsylvania RR was rejected, it was a foregone conclusion that he would not stop where he was. He next resorted to the courts, and there appeared upon the scene a motley collection of judges, most of them more or less a disgrace to the legal profession. Of these, the most notorious was Judge Barnard. He was a judge of the state court in the

First District (Manhattan). There were eight districts in New York State, each with four judges (except the First, which had five). There are two important points concerning these state courts to be borne in mind. The first is that a judge held powers in equity throughout the state, not just in his own district. The second is that judges were elected, and the judicial system was therefore open to the same abuses which attached to other elected officials, notably legislators, in the 'gilded age'. These were the conditions that gave rise to the unbecoming sight of injunctions being flung about in all directions by various different judges in the conflicting interests of those with whom they were more or less corruptly associated.

Vanderbilt was out to corner Drew, and no one realized better than he that such a task would be extremely demanding. It was not too difficult to acquire Erie stock in the open market, given the millions that Vanderbilt could deploy, provided it could be done quietly. But assuming that part of the operation could be completed successfully, it was necessary to ensure that Drew was not in a position to stage a counter-coup, as he had done in 1866. That particular transaction had never been settled, and Vanderbilt seized on it as a rope with which to tie the wily treasurer down. The agreeable Judge Barnard granted an order restraining Drew from reclaiming the $3.5 million loan to the company and from forcing a settlement of his claims against the company.

Stock being traded on the street, New York, 1864

Another suit requested the removal of Drew from his post as treasurer.

During these hearings a major obstacle to Vanderbilt's plans, of just the sort he had feared, was revealed. It consisted of a mountain of Erie stock the existence of which had been unsuspected. Drew and his associates had been busy.

A recent statute of New York State empowered a railroad company to issue new stock of its own in exchange for the stock of any other railroad which it took under lease. No doubt Drew and his friends had a hand in the passing of this statute which, as events proved, made it fairly simple for a company to increase its capital stock, a process otherwise forbidden by law. Drew and his associates had acquired, for a paltry sum, a useless railroad called the Buffalo, Bradford and Pittsburgh (though the citizens of either Buffalo or Pittsburgh would have had to travel a long way to find it). A complicated transaction followed in which Drew and his friends adopted different roles for appropriate occasions, acting now as proprietors of the newly acquired railroad, now as directors of the Erie and, as it were, making bargains with themselves in which both sides benefited. The upshot was that the Erie directors leased the new road for 499 years and took over $2 million of its bonds (payable to themselves), issued by the new owners (the Erie directors wearing different hats), and these were exchanged for convertible Erie bonds. The Buffalo, Bradford and Pittsburgh stock was also exchanged for Erie stock. This, plus the convertible bonds, represented a sizeable new amount of Erie stock – a blow to Vanderbilt.

However, on March 3 Judge Barnard issued his injunction restraining the Erie Board from any new issue of capital stock and also forbidding it guaranteeing the bonds of any connecting railroad. In addition, Drew and his associates were restrained from any dealing in Erie stock until Drew returned to the company the stock involved both in the 1866 transaction and in the Buffalo, Bradford and Pittsburgh exchange. Drew's guns appeared to be spiked. His whole operation had for years depended basically on his ability to issue new Erie stock more or less at will. This avenue was now closed. Erie stock had been rising steadily, and Drew had been selling short. A Vanderbilt corner looked likely to succeed on March 10, when the injunction was due to be served.

But Drew had not been inactive. The Erie being short of funds as usual, he had advanced another loan on security of convertible Erie bonds. (The company was not allowed to issue new capital stock if the price was below par, but it was allowed to issue convertible bonds to secure a loan at any price; when these regulations were framed it was not foreseen that people like Drew would employ bond issues to increase capital stock.) At a secret meeting of the Erie executive committee, $10 million of convertible bonds were issued, of which half were immediately bought by Drew and turned into stock in a matter of minutes. There was now a potential avalanche of Erie stock poised ready to swamp Vanderbilt in a flood of paper.

But before the second half of this latest issue could be brought into play, Judge Barnard, whittling away bad-temperedly at a piece of wood and littering his judicial bench with shavings, stopped it by his injunction. Nevertheless, stock certificates were prepared for instant issue in place of the bonds.

On the morning of March 9 the stock certificates, already made out, were in the hands of the company secretary. A messenger taking them from one office to another was intercepted on his way by Jim Fisk, an Erie director and a member of the brokerage firm in whose name the certificates were written. 'I'll take those,' said Fisk, and made off with them. The certificates were 'lost' and therefore beyond the power of injunctions and, since the owners were making no complaint, Fisk could hardly be charged with theft. Needless to say, they soon appeared on the market, and it was difficult to say who, by issuing them, was guilty of contempt of court. Their effect was to bring the price of Erie stock tumbling down. Vanderbilt's corner was defeated.

All this time court injunctions were flying back and forth as thick, though not as pure, as the driven snow. The story reads 'like some monstrous parody of the forms of law,' wrote C. F. Adams, 'some Saturnalia of bench and bar', with judges actually employing private detectives to spy on witnesses.

On the morning of March 11 the Erie directors heard that officers were on their way to arrest them for contempt of court. Hastily stuffing their files into bags and parcels, they fled for the New Jersey ferry. One man is said to have carried $6

Fisk as maître de ballet. *His lavish theatrical productions were largely designed to amuse his mistress, though of course he immensely enjoyed the role of impresario*

million in greenbacks (Federal treasury notes) in a hired cab, while two who delayed were arrested. Setting up their headquarters in a hotel in Jersey City, Drew and his associates proceeded to have the Erie incorporated in New Jersey. This was a move of minor strategic importance; the real battle would still have to be fought in New York. They had bodyguards at every door and even stationed armed men in boats on the river. Nor were these sensational precautions idle, for a gang of toughs appeared from across the Hudson, apparently charged with kidnapping the Erie directors and carrying them back by force into the jurisdiction of the New York courts. The news of this episode, not unnaturally, caused a sensation no less than the original flight of the Erie directors and the Erie assets, but probably too much has been made of it. If there was a genuine plot to capture Drew and company, then it was very feebly planned and it is hard to believe that a man like Vanderbilt could have had any connection with such a badly botched scheme.

Vanderbilt certainly had reason for feeling bitter. The Erie directors had relieved him of about $7 million and he was loaded up with Erie shares bought at far above their current price, which he could not unload for fear of causing a panic; for the same reason, moreover, he would be compelled to buy yet more stock if Drew managed to manufacture any. The struggle had placed a strain on even his resources, and he was not far from the brink of ruin, but he carried on as usual, displaying all his normal zest at the whist table.

In one sense it was Drew, rather than the defeated Vanderbilt, who suffered most. The sensational events of March were too much for Drew who, for all his plots and schemes, had little relish for a knock-out fight, and bitterly resented having to cross the river on Sundays only (when he could not be arrested) in order to see his family and go to church. Increasingly, the Erie leadership was falling into the hands of two younger directors, Jay Gould and James Fisk, Jr.

Jay Gould remains something of an enigma. In an age of unprincipled financial operators, he was possibly the most brilliant – and possibly the most unprincipled. Despite his long and close relationship with Fisk, he was a retiring man, fond of his family and little interested in the vulgar and spectacular entertainments so beloved by his partner. Undoubtedly he liked making money, but making money is seldom satisfying for long as an end in itself, and Gould was more than just a gambler. The imponderability of his deepest motives still lends some mystery to his character. Though he did some good work for railroads later in his career, he was not really interested in problems of transportation. He was occasionally capable of generosity but in general his business relationships were 'sharp to the point of knavery'; he was said to have been the cause of one suicide very early in his business career, certainly some later, and he was himself, despite his bodyguards, the victim of physical assault on more than one occasion.

Jay Gould

Jim Fisk was a quite different character. Less capable than Gould, he was equally unprincipled, but there was not much doubt about his motives. Daring and impulsive, he enjoyed being a celebrity, and spent his more or less ill-gotten gains on lavish display and amusement. He liked to cut a dash, and succeeded in doing so to his own satisfaction, though barred from the clubs and drawing rooms of the more respectable among the rich. In a different age, he might never have amounted to anything more than a successful travelling salesman (as he once had been) and he was even less interested than Gould in improved transport, the public welfare, industrial progress, or any nonsense of that sort. He wanted a good time, he had one, and he was the first to say so; his good humour was his one endearing characteristic. Even the record of his testimony before a Congressional committee is genuinely amusing – though that was probably the only genuine thing about it.

The Gilbertian activities of counsel and judges resulted in Judge Barnard appointing a receiver for the Erie in the person of Peter B. Sweeney, a Tammany leader and close associate of William Tweed, the corrupt 'boss' of New York politics. Since all the company's assets were in New Jersey, there was nothing for the receiver to receive; nevertheless, Judge Barnard awarded him $150,000 for his non-receiving. The question of the Erie directors' contempt of court was also settled later very amicably, the highest individual penalty imposed being $10. This less than draconian punishment may have resulted from a spirit of humane forgiveness descending upon the soul of Judge Barnard, or from the fact that his good friends Messrs Tweed and Sweeney had become directors of the Erie

Railroad and bosom pals of Jay Gould and Jim Fisk.

Meanwhile, the battle moved to Albany, the seat of the state government. Gould, who was now running Erie strategy, had a bill introduced which, among other useful things, would legalize the contested $10 million bond issue, but it was defeated in the Assembly (the lower house) by eighty-three votes to thirty-two. A senate committee also reported adversely, the deciding vote being cast by a senator whom Gould believed 'bought'; so he was, but bought twice over, and Vanderbilt had paid the larger price. It appeared that Vanderbilt's interests were too powerful in the capital, so Gould decided to go to Albany himself—the Commander-in-Chief forsaking staff headquarters in order to take command of the front line. He went well armed too, with $500,000 of Erie money. However, no sooner had he arrived than he was arrested on the writ for contempt of court. He appeared in court in New York City and was put in charge of an officer who was ordered not to let the accused out of his sight until the deferred hearings took place a few days later. Gould at once returned to Albany; the officer, interpreting his orders literally, saw no reason why his charge should not go anywhere, provided that he travelled in the same carriage himself. Back in his Albany hotel, Gould was suddenly taken ill. His symptoms were far from obvious to the lay observer, but his doctor pronounced him quite unfit to travel to New York. The patient did, however, manage to get himself to the Legislature without difficulty, and he proved strong enough to entertain its members until a late hour.

There was little doubt in the public's mind that corruption existed in the Legislature on a large scale, but investigations and inquiries never managed to turn up any concrete evidence of scandal. While the Erie's bill was going through, however, rumours of massive bribery by both sides were growing too strong to be ignored. One day, an obscure and elderly Assemblyman named Glenn announced in great excitement that he had just been offered money for his vote on the Erie bill. At last, a substantial, reliable charge had been made. An investigating committee was appointed, but found that Mr Glenn had been the victim of a practical joke. Someone had told him that a peddler hanging around the Capitol was an agent for the vote-buyers. He had approached him and at length elicited what he thought was an offer for his vote. The

Albany in 1837, after
W. H. Bartlett

names of other Assemblymen were mentioned. The investigating committee found the whole affair to be no more than a silly prank: the gullible Mr Glenn was censured and immediately resigned; the peddler was arrested. The affair fizzled out, and with it the tense, inflated balloon of rumoured graft was pricked. No one cared to make any more allegations of vote-buying and that, perhaps, is why the incident was engineered in the first place.

Opinion in the Legislature began to turn in favour of the Erie, influenced by the dispensation of Gould's money but also, perhaps, by popular antipathy to the looming monopoly of Vanderbilt, which Gould and his agents made the most of. A new bill was introduced which, in essentials, scarcely differed from the earlier bill defeated in the Assembly. The Assemblymen rubbed their hands in anticipation of rich hand-outs from the contestants, and members who had not been seen in Albany for months hastened to take their part in the debate. But then Vanderbilt suddenly withdrew his opposition. The bill sailed through by 101 votes to six. The legislators, thwarted of their graft, vented their anger at Vanderbilt by rushing through a couple of railway regulation acts whose sole purpose was to injure his interests.

Obviously Vanderbilt had made a deal with the Erie, though its nature was not revealed until some time later. Drew, who had never relished the battle with his old rival, believed that the 'Commodore', as he had been known since his shipping days, would be prepared to settle. The gist of their agreement was that the Erie agreed to take back a large quantity of Vanderbilt's Erie stock at a reasonable price.

Various other parties had to be taken care of, including the Boston group who received their $4 million of Erie securities for the virtually worthless bonds of the Boston, Hartford and Erie RR. The whole settlement cost the Erie something like $10 million, and everyone had reason to feel satisfied with the arrangements – except, of course, the genuine investors among the public.

Gould and Fisk maintained that they had opposed the settlement, and later took to the courts to recover some money from Vanderbilt. They may not have made much personal profit from the settlement, but they were left in almost undisputed control of one asset which had already proved priceless – the Erie Railroad. During the next few years they proceeded to show that they knew every trick that 'Uncle Dan'l' had ever pulled and a few more besides. Gould was elected president, with Fisk as comptroller of accounts, and lost no time in issuing another $10 million in convertible bonds. Half of these were swiftly turned into stock, confirming Vanderbilt's rueful observation that he could easily afford to buy the Erie but he could not buy the printing press. In the first four months of Gould's presidency, the stock of the company was increased from $34 million to $58 million, causing such a severe currency shortage that the Federal treasury was forced to intervene. Vanderbilt kept a finger in the Erie pie, but a successful corner disposed of Daniel Drew, who had once used the technique so skilfully himself. Drew lived until 1879, but he spent his last years as a bankrupt.

Gould and Fisk prospered. The alliance with Tweed and his cronies was solid; British investors bought Erie stock in large quantities and the stock bought back from Vanderbilt was resold without loss. Gould justified every issue of new stock by the need to prevent Vanderbilt getting a monopoly, and never stopped to wonder if the unfortunate Erie stockholders might not consider a Vanderbilt takeover preferable to being fleeced by their current directors.

Management of the company continued in a scandalous manner. The courts again were busy, the company was tottering on the edge of disaster and a receiver was appointed – who else but Jay Gould himself? Another court meanwhile appointed a neutral receiver, but he was prevented from gaining access to the Erie offices by Jim Fisk's bully boys. At

Nast's view of a Tammany 'cabinet' under 'President' Tweed. Jim Fisk's celebrated steamboats earn him the post of Secretary of the Navy

least two other judges were in the field with their own candidates for the receivership. For a while trading in Erie stock was banned by the Stock Exchange, but nonetheless it continued in the street. Once Fisk travelled to New Jersey disguised as an old man to avoid a writ being served on him. Another time it was rumoured that the Erie chiefs had fled to Canada in a coach stacked to the roof with money. The railroad itself grew ever rustier and more unreliable, while the Gould-

Pike's Opera House in New York, headquarters of the Erie Railroad

Fisk combine made millions out of it. The steel rails, purchase of which Gould was for ever citing as the reason for expenditure, seldom seemed to materialize.

Fat, fair and not yet forty, Jim Fisk, with his perky waxed moustache, was having a marvellous time. He and Gould purchased a redundant opera house, an ostentatious white marble edifice in Manhattan Baroque, which served as headquarters of the Erie. They bought it in their own names with Erie money and then leased it to the company at $75,000 a year – a typical example of how to have one's cake and eat it. The Erie offices were reached by a grand carved staircase leading to a pair of huge doors with a tessellated marble hall beyond – all stained glass, Pompeian frescoes and glass chandeliers. The offices were decorated in Fisk's most ostentatious style, with engraved mirrors, silk hangings and marble statues. The company safe ascended seven storeys from its granite base at ground level to the roof: it was said that if the building burned down the safe would remain unscathed. In the theatre itself, Fisk dabbled with operatic productions, partly to please his mistress, a good-looking though heavy-jowelled gold-digger with theatrical aspirations but without the requisite talents.

The complex of buildings behind the Opera House was also owned by the Erie. It contained Fisk's private apartments and his stables – fifteen horses and eight carriages of various types. He had, too, a couple of enormous and lavishly decorated ferry steamers, named the *James Fisk Jr* and the *Jay Gould*. He liked to dress up as an admiral and see the passengers on board, though he hardly knew one end of a ship from the other.

Gould, grave and silent, concerned himself with railroad business. He nearly beat the New York Central and the Pennsylvania RR to a direct route into Chicago, and he made a satisfying profit by outsmarting the Commodore. In an effort to secure the monopoly of the transport of cattle from the west, Vanderbilt fixed a freight rate far below the actual cost. When Gould heard of this, he bought all the cattle in the Chicago stockyards and shipped them to New York via the New York Central, at a good profit. 'If the Commodore wants to make me a present,' he said, 'I can't stop him.'

In 1868 valuable stone quarries were located near the Erie, and Gould tried to buy them. The proprietor did not want to sell, but Gould pointed out that if he did not, the Erie would refuse to carry the stone – whereupon he gave in. A new company was formed consisting of the original proprietor and members of the Erie ring, including Tweed, to quarry the stone and ship it to New York City, which, thanks to the good offices of Boss Tweed, bought the product for building purposes at a very high price.

An obscure shareholder wondered what was happening to all the money – over $50 million – that Gould and Fisk had added to the Erie stock, and he brought a suit for a full accounting. Suddenly he found the case transferred to Manhattan district, where Judge Barnard presided. The Judge issued an injunction against his proceedings, then fined him for contempt of court when he attempted to find evidence to support his case. This deterred others from needlessly disturbing the business activities of Messrs Gould and Fisk. The editor of a Massachusetts newspaper who had periodically attacked the combination in print was arrested on a visit to New York with his sick wife and kept in jail overnight despite efforts by his friends to bail him out. This incident caused a sensation, not least because this victim of Jim Fisk's control of sheriff and judge was a socially prominent newspaper editor.

The most audacious scheme that Gould ever dreamed up was the notorious attempt to corner gold in 1869, which led to the extraordinary scenes of Black Friday, September 24. 'Of all financial operations,' wrote Henry Adams, 'cornering gold is the most brilliant and the most dangerous, and possibly the very hazard and splendour of the attempt were the reasons of

147

its fascination to Mr Jay Gould's fancy.' Briefly, the operation depended on a tacit alliance with the Federal treasury, which contained more than sufficient gold to defeat a corner if it released it. Gould had a link with President Grant through the President's brother-in-law, and on visits to New York Grant received the full blast of Fisk's florid hospitality. Gould felt that he was safe in assuming that the Treasury would not sell, but, even if it did, he calculated he would learn about it soon enough to sell while the price was still high. In fact the Treasury, at the last moment, did sell. Gould, at the centre of his spider's web, sitting on a stool in the back room of a broker's office tearing bits of paper into little pieces, started to sell his holdings while Fisk, who was not in his partner's confidence, continued to buy, bidding the price up to an unparalleled 162, amid scenes of frantic hysteria in the Gold Room, next door to the Stock Exchange on Broad Street. Thus, though the corner was defeated, Gould managed to unload his gold, which amounted to about $50 million. Although events had not turned out as he had planned, at the end of the day he was $3 million to the good. Fisk was left with contracts that he could not possibly fulfil, but he wriggled out of his difficulties by producing a copy of a letter from a broker named Belden, a former partner, which appeared to show that all Fisk's purchases of gold had been made on behalf of Belden.

Of the many scandalous episodes that punctuated the history of the Erie under the management of the Gould ring, the most sensational was the attempt to gain control of the Albany and Susquehanna Railroad. This was a local line, completed early in 1869 after a long history of construction difficulties, which ran between Albany and Binghampton, where it connected with the Erie. From the latter's point of view it offered a number of strategic advantages, and Gould and Fisk set out to acquire it by gaining control of enough stock to give them a majority in the election of directors, due annually in September. Their chief opponent was Joseph H. Ramsay, 'father' of the railroad and president of the board. A certain amount of stock was available on the open market, and Erie purchases in the summer of 1869 rapidly sent its value up from about twenty to sixty-five. There was also a group of directors in conflict with Ramsay, and their holdings, added to the Erie purchases, represented a considerable portion, but not a majority, of the stock. It appeared that the balance was held by the towns along the route of the railroad. This stock, however, was subject to certain restrictions designed to preserve municipal interests from the depredations of officials who might be tempted to sell it to private owners. It could only be sold at par value (100) and for cash down.

In the situation of the railroad before the battle for control began, that was pie in the sky, but soon Gould's agents appeared in the towns concerned with bags of money offering to buy the stock on the terms laid down. It was a very tempting offer, but Ramsay's agents were also busy, warning the people of the dire consequences likely for their railroad if Gould and his friends got their hands on it. Some towns did sell, but Ramsay himself then entered the contest, sending the price so high that Gould and Fisk decided they would have to acquire the stock by less expensive methods. The solution they evolved characteristically avoided a direct and obvious infringement of the letter of the law while destroying the spirit of it. They offered their personal bonds to buy the stock of the towns still holding out, at their price, *after* the election, provided their representatives would vote with the Erie *in* the elections. Despite the dubious reliability of such bonds, the towns agreed to this arrangement.

Ramsay was not beaten yet. There still remained 12,000 shares authorized but not subscribed for in the Albany and Susquehanna's treasury. With the election imminent, Ramsay got together some friends who agreed to subscribe for 9,500 of these shares for an initial payment of ten per cent, which Ramsay would provide. This was a move of the kind associated with unscrupulous operators like Gould and Fisk; in making it, Ramsay implicitly acknowledged that he too was prepared to live by the law of the jungle.

The contest was transferred to the courts. The Erie ring sought an injunction to prevent Ramsay's friends voting the new stock. Ramsay gained an injunction against the transfer of some of the municipal shares to the Erie. The Erie obtained an order stopping Ramsay from acting as a director of the railroad. Since the board was divided equally between the supporters of Ramsay and those of the Erie, this move gave the latter a majority, and all they now had to do was to call a directors' meeting at which they would be able to get hold of the company's books and make such transfers of stock as would give them clear control.

The meeting took place in Albany on Thursday, August 5, two days before the last permissible date for stock transfers before the election. There were angry scenes, and the police were called in. When the meeting resumed next day, Ramsay's lawyers turned up with injunctions against four of the opposing directors, forbidding them to act. Retaliatory enjoinders prevented anyone doing anything, and with the management in tatters, both sides demanded the appointment of a receiver, the Erie side recommending Jim Fisk for the job. Judge Barnard's signature appeared on the requisite order, though at the time he appears to have been seventy miles away at the bedside of his dying mother in Poughkeepsie, and Fisk, accompanied by a small army of lawyers and roughhouse boys, left New York for Albany on the night train. Arriving at the railroad's offices next morning, they found the building in the possession of the Ramsay interests, who had had their own candidate appointed as receiver by an Albany judge.

Fisk demanded the company books, which had in fact been removed from the offices secretly on the night of August 5, and when he attempted to enter the room where they were kept, a brief tussle took place, and the Erie men were pushed down the stairs and out on to the street. 'I'll be damned,' said Jim Fisk, puffing hard, 'I'll be damned.' His dignity promptly suffered another blow when an Albany policeman, confused, bewildered but deciding that Fisk was the chief instigator of the riot, arrested him. He was released almost at once, and returned to the Susquehanna offices, greeting his opponents quite amiably and suggesting to Ramsay that they should play a round of cards to decide who should own the railroad.

This solution having been rejected, the courts were again brought into play. Some useful orders issued by the ubiquitous Judge Barnard, who still seemed capable of attending his mother's deathbed in Poughkeepsie while he was signing orders in New York, arrived by telegraph, one of them putting the local sheriff at the orders of the Erie receiver – Fisk. The sheriff was reluctant to act on orders issued by this means, certainly a novelty then, but he accompanied Fisk to the railroad offices where a truce was arranged: both sides agreed to do nothing until after the weekend.

Fisk was a favourite butt of the cartoonists, but this, he said, was his favourite representation of himself, and he ordered a large number of copies of the publication in which it appeared

After consultations in New York, the Fisk party returned to Albany on Sunday night to find that Ramsay was again one step ahead of them. The Albany judge had dissolved Judge Barnard's injunctions and cited Fisk for contempt of court. It was beginning to look as though the opposition in Albany was too strong for the Erie group, but, as Fisk remarked, a railroad has two ends.

The Albany judge's orders which in effect put the railroad into the hands of the pro-Ramsay receiver were put on the train leaving Albany at 8 am on Monday morning, to be communicated to all the stations on the line to Binghampton. The train was due to terminate at that town at 3 pm. But there was an even faster method of communication – the telegraph. Thus the Erie group were able to get in touch with Binghampton (which, unlike Albany, was Erie territory anyway), and though the writ of the Albany judge scotched them most of the way down the line, at Binghampton the – telegraphed – writ of Judge Barnard ruled. The sheriff there proceeded to take possession of all the property of the railroad, including a train just getting up steam for its scheduled departure for Albany. There were also three locomotives at Binghampton. The sheriff took possession of two and was on his way to claim the third when an official sympathetic to the Ramsay management contrived to switch the points so that the engine on which the sheriff was travelling was diverted into a siding, while the locomotive he was after slipped past and escaped into Albany territory.

Now the two ends of the line were in the hands of the two opposing groups. At the same time, the sheriffs from Albany and Binghampton, armed with the conflicting writs of the rival judges, were both entrained, one heading south, the other north, and likely to meet with a mighty clash somewhere not far north of Binghampton. However, at Harpersville, twenty-five miles north of Binghampton, the Albany train stopped. All other traffic had come to a standstill on orders from Albany (the feelings of any innocent members of the public attempting to travel on the Albany and Susqhehanna on this day are unrecorded), but a special train with 150 brawny mechanics from the Albany machine shops was despatched southward. The Binghampton train, carrying a dozen or so Erie men as well as the sheriff, was still proceeding north, stopping at each station to turn out the Albany men and replace them with Erie officials, according to Judge Barnard's orders. From the Albany offices came a warning that they proceeded at their own risk; nevertheless, they continued, creeping slowly through the darkness (for by this time the hour was late) until they reached Bainbridge, where their locomotive suddenly gave a slight lurch and slid off the rails. The Albany party, waiting in a siding, had booby-trapped the main line, and while the Erie men were stranded at Bainbridge, the Albany train moved out on to the main track behind them and set off south, towards Binghampton, stopping at every station to reverse the process just carried out by the Erie men and restore the Albany employees to their posts. About fifteen miles from Binghampton they came to a long tunnel, where they found a hastily assembled band of Erie men, carrying sticks. For several hours nothing happened, except that each group, on either side of the tunnel, received reinforcements from special trains coming up behind them while they awaited orders from their rival headquarters in Albany. There, Jim Fisk was commanding the Erie forces from his hotel suite. At 7 am the Erie men received the order to advance. Their train chugged warily through the tunnel and, emerging unscathed, kept going on the steep downward gradient through the cutting beyond. As it rounded a sharp curve, it met the Albany train coming up. At this stage the Erie men outnumbered their opponents by nearly two to one, but besides being less well-armed (some of the Albany bunch had guns), they were not motivated by the feelings of loyalty and outrage that spurred Ramsay's men onward. It rapidly became obvious that the Albany train was not going to stop. The Erie train tried to reverse, but it was hard to get a grip on the steep gradient, and before it could get going the Albany locomotive slammed straight into it. The Erie locomotive, shorn of its cow-catcher, headlights and smokestack, received a blow which gave it just the start it needed, and it continued precipitately backwards. Both parties had poured out of the carriages, but the Erie men, already shocked by the unexpected aggression of their opponents, and hearing a few gun shots (one bullet went through the engine cab), were in no mood for a fight, and ran for it. Some of them clambered back on the train now fast vanishing into the tunnel.

The Albany locomotive had been derailed in the collision, but Ramsay's men managed to get it back on the tracks and set off in pursuit. On the far side of the tunnel the Erie men rallied, but before a serious fight could begin, news came that soldiers were approaching – the militia had been called out to stop the riot. The Albany men overturned a freight car to block the line and retired through the tunnel once more, eventually reaching Albany where they were greeted as heroes. Public opinion all along the railroad was strongly for Ramsay, and the Governor of New York, hastily summoned back from vacation, threatened to impose martial law if there were any further outbreaks of violence in the region.

On Tuesday evening Fisk made another attempt, after dark, to force access to the company's offices in Albany, but, finding Ramsay's men on guard, he tried a little bribery instead. Neither method got him into the building, and to his annoyance he was once more arrested, and charged with endeavouring to gain control of the railroad by force. Released on bail, he departed hastily for New York. Thereupon, Judge Barnard had Ramsay and his chief associates arrested for contempt of court.

Things had reached an impasse. The Governor insisted that the two sides should find some way of agreement, and, when they told him they could not do so, he ordered the railroad to be taken over by state officials pending a settlement. Arguments dragged on in the courts until 'at last, the battle of the judges died away in a faint rumble of evidence, affidavits, explanations, and orders, and then was heard of no more'.

The election drew nigh. The Erie men were still anxious to have a look at the stock books, which would reveal the strength or weakness of their voting position, but Ramsay had hidden them away – one hiding place is said to have been a tomb in the Albany cemetery – and they were only smuggled back into the company offices the night before the election in a basket let down from a third-floor window at the rear of the building. But the Erie ring struck a decisive blow when they managed by a legal manoeuvre depending largely on bluff to get hold of a substantial quantity of stock held as security for loans to the company, which was voted in their interest. The day of the election provided new scenes of argument, accusation, writs and counter-writs. Fisk provided a gang of his toughs with proxies so they could attend. The Erie group had more votes, but to achieve this majority they had indulged in any number of questionable activities, including having Ramsay arrested at the very moment when his presence was, in his own interests, most vital, leaving his opponents in possession of the field. The outcome was that both sides declared their own list of directors elected, and the situation remained as before. The railroad itself continued to be operated by the state, and the Governor called for the possession of the company to be decided once and for all by the courts.

An action brought by the New York State Attorney-General was tried before an independent judge in Rochester in November. Gould and Fisk, at this time much occupied with their dealings in gold, proposed a compromise to Ramsay in which the Erie would lease the Albany and Susqhehanna on fairly generous terms. But Ramsay would not deal at any price. He was confident of getting the judgement at Rochester, and a few months later his confidence was justified by Justice Smith's decision that the election of the pro-Erie board was 'irregular, fraudulent and void'.

That was not quite the end of the matter. The Erie counsel attempted to overturn the judgement through appeals, and it was Ramsay himself who brought the business to an end. Having fought off the Erie successfully, he turned around and leased his railroad to the powerful Hudson and Delaware Canal Company, an organization with which Gould and Fisk did not care to tangle.

Though they had other interests too, Gould and Fisk continued to milk the Erie after the Albany and Susqhehanna affair. Fisk was also busy with his theatrical productions, his steamboats and his trotting horses. Now and then he visited Boston, where his rather obscure wife preferred to live. Fisk had a reputation as a womanizer; it was said that his stage productions were promoted chiefly to supply him with a choice of chorus girls, but latterly at least he remained faithful to his mistress, 'Dolly', whom he had set up in a comfortable house where he spent more time than he did in his own, relatively modest, domestic quarters. Eventually, however, Jim and Dolly fell out. The trouble concerned a good-looking business associate of Fisk named Ed Stokes. Finding himself cut out of Dolly's affections by Stokes, Fisk not unnaturally cut

The murder of Jim Fisk at the Grand Central Hotel, from a contemporary illustrated newspaper

'Dead Men Tell No Tales' – one of Nast's brilliant cartoons, showing Gould (in front), Tweed (with handkerchief) and others mourning over Fisk's grave, watched by a frustrated figure of Justice

Stokes out of a profitable oil-refining business in which they were associated. Legal actions followed and personal revelations that would have been mortally embarrassing to anyone but Fisk were published in the press. Stokes had conceived a burning hatred for Fisk, and the final scene of the sordid drama was played out in the Grand Central Hotel on a November day in 1871. As Fisk began climbing the long staircase on his way to visit a friend, Stokes appeared at the top with a pistol in his hand. 'Now I've got you,' he snarled, and shot his enemy in the stomach.

Fisk lived for some time, long enough to miss the diamond pin, big as a cherry, which someone had removed from his shirtfront, and to be visited by Gould, anxious to prevent any damaging private papers getting into the wrong hands, and other old associates, including 'Boss' Tweed, whose reign had ended; he was out on bail pending the trial in which he was sentenced to twelve years for his swindles. Jim remarked that he was sorry so many of Tweed's friends had deserted him; he feared he was about to lose another. He died the next day and was buried in his hometown of Brattleboro, Vermont, where a moderately imposing marble memorial marks his final resting place.

Gould remained in control of the Erie Railroad until 1874, when British stockholders, eventually becoming exasperated, combined with reformist groups to oust him. The company was already bankrupt, and the new management was forced within a few months to admit that it could not meet its financial obligations; the Erie went into receivership.

Meanwhile, Gould moved his area of operations to the west. He virtually controlled the Union Pacific for a while, reaping about $10 million when he sold out, and built up a large railroad system on Vanderbilt's pattern in the south-west. Like Hill, Harriman and other great railway barons, his career showed that the real profits were to be made not from building pioneer lines, but from taking over such lines when they were in dire financial plight and consolidating them in a growing railroad empire. His most valuable gift of timing – acquiring assets at low prices – never left him. Always tough and unscrupulous, Gould cannot be dismissed as a mere bandit; his operations overall frequently led to greater efficiency. Among his other interests, he controlled the Western Union Telegraph Company and the elevated railway in New York City and owned the *New York World*. Silent and friendless to the end, he died in 1892, bequeathing his empire to his son.

6 The Last of the Empire Builders

Depressions, which regularly punctuated the history of the American economy in the nineteenth century, were not necessarily disastrous events for all concerned. The slumps that brought ruin to many also brought the opportunity of future prosperity to others, who were able to buy both plant and materials at rock-bottom prices. In the depression that followed the slump of 1873, for instance, the basis was laid for Carnegie's steel business, for Armour's meat-packing empire, and for Rockefeller's oil monopoly. By bankrupting the Northern Pacific, among other railroads, the slump also gave an obscure businessman from St Paul, Minnesota, the chance to enter the railroad business.

James Hill arrived in St Paul in 1856 at the age of eighteen. He had been born in Canada at the tiny settlement of Rockwood, forty miles west of Toronto, and was of Scotch-Irish descent. His mental ability persuaded his father to send him to a private school run by a devoted Quaker teacher who aroused in him a lifelong interest in literature and encouraged him to follow a sober, industrious way of life. Though bookish, the boy also took to the outdoor life of a pioneer settlement – shooting and fishing becoming his favourite forms of relaxation. An accident with a bow and arrow he was making for his younger brother deprived him permanently of the sight of one eye, though the handicap was never apparent to those ignorant of it, and ended the family's hopes that he would become a doctor. A few years later, when he was fourteen, his father died and his formal education came to an end. For four years he helped support the family by working in a village store, then he left home to seek his fortune. He seems to have returned only once or twice.

The young Hill had vague ideas of going to India, but, after some wandering around, he settled, more or less by chance, in St Paul, where he was to live the rest of his life. When he arrived there, St Paul, at the head of Mississippi navigation, was no older than he was. The total population was less than 5,000, though rising fast, and there was not yet a single flour mill across the river in what became Minneapolis. In the territory of Minnesota altogether (a somewhat larger area than the modern state) there lived hardly more than 150,000 people of European descent, mainly in the valleys of the big rivers. Beyond, in the woods and prairies, and on some of the richest farm land in the world, the Sioux and the Chippewa roamed comparatively undisturbed, though they were soon to be pushed out by the white man. The Red River valley, which was to play so important a role in the early stages of Hill's empire-building, was almost deserted. Its earliest settlements were just beginning in the area around what is now Winnipeg, on the Canadian side of the border.

The young Canadian (Hill did not become an American citizen until 1880) soon found a job as a shipping clerk. It was a rugged existence; the young clerk had to take a hand in loading cargo on the rapidly multiplying steamboats and on occasion had to jump into the river to help save a boy from drowning, or repulse drunken Irishmen with his fists. One night he sat up with a friend who was ill, reading a book about engineering. Asked if he intended to become an engineer, he replied that he was 'a young man yet, and a little knowledge about engineering may prove useful one day'.

His blind eye kept him out of the Civil War, and in 1865 he went into business for himself as a shipping agent, numbering among his clients the Northwestern Packet Company, which connected with the Chicago, Milwaukee and St Paul Railroad and the Illinois Central.

James J. Hill was on the short side, but stocky in build; in later years he tipped the scales at 200 lb. In a large, blunt-featured face which radiated confidence, his rather narrow eyes, both seeming to gaze with equal shrewdness, were set above broad expanses of cheek; as early as his thirties, most of his hair was gone or going, but he compensated for this with a heavy beard which, in the elderly, grizzled, railroad magnate, gave him an appearance that, even allowing for the rigidity of nineteenth century photographs, was decidedly severe. He was, nevertheless, humorous and high-spirited, amiable though tough and given to occasional outbursts of rage, imaginative, intelligent and energetic. These qualities, seasoned by ambition, were revealed in the rapid expansion of his business interests during the next few years, which included transactions of many kinds in goods and transportation.

In 1866, Hill married a girl of Irish descent and embarked upon a life of relatively untroubled domesticity, during which ten children were born (all except one were alive at his death). Hill appears to have been a devoted family man, and though business usually came first, he was never much tempted by the worldly pleasures which his industrial eminence later put in his way. His wife was Roman Catholic, but Hill, though he contributed lavishly to Catholic charities, never joined the Church. On the subject of his religious feelings his biographers are, no doubt appropriately, silent.

Hill's railroad career began at the age of forty, by which time he was already a prominent figure in St Paul. He had achieved, indeed surpassed, the ambition he had formulated twelve years earlier of making $100,000. Among his diverse activities, he seldom missed an opportunity of profit. For example, when a firm of iron founders went bankrupt, he bought their assets at the sheriff's sale for $3,600. He had observed, lying about in the firm's yard, a large quantity of scrap iron, which he sold for $6,600. He sold the mould patterns for $2,000, the building for $4,400 and the machinery for $1,760. Although all this took about two years, it represented a very handsome profit on the initial investment.

He was already involved in transport. In the summer months his steamboats chugged precariously up and down the Red River (a Red River steamboat, it was said, had to be capable of navigating in a heavy dew), their business increasing, while Hill became acquainted with the problems and potentials of transport in the north-west. Almost as

St Paul in 1857 (soon after Hill's arrival), looking towards the Capitol (since replaced by a grander building)

James J. Hill in 1910

important were his operations in the fuel business which, accompanied by a thorough study of the coal resources of the region, were to pay dividends in the future. The north-west is very cold: winter temperatures in parts of North Dakota are regularly lower than those of the North Pole, and Hill was one of the first to see that, just as railroads would replace steamboats, coal would replace wood. This ability to look ahead, not just to next month or next year but to the next decade or the next generation, was of more importance in his success than the legendary 'Jim Hill's luck' which people often quoted. Meanwhile, he did well by supplying the St Paul and Pacific Railroad with wood fuel, though increasingly it was the transportation side of his business that absorbed Hill's interest and time. Settlers, mainly from Scandinavia and Germany, were flowing into the north-west at an ever-growing rate, and the need for better transportation, especially transportation that operated throughout the year, was becoming increasingly evident.

In 1864 the Northern Pacific was chartered to build a railroad from Lake Superior across the north-west to Portland, Oregon. Nothing much was done until 1870, when Jay Cooke of Philadelphia undertook to raise the $100 million and more necessary to complete the work. Cooke was a remarkable man who had made his reputation and his fortune by financing loans to the Union government during the Civil War. For a year or two, the Northern Pacific under his leadership made considerable progress. By 1873 the railroad ran from Lake Superior across Minnesota to the Red River at Moorhead and westward as far as Bismarck, but the panic of 1873 made Northern Pacific bonds, with which construction had been financed, unsaleable. Jay Cooke's company was forced to close down in 1874, and the Northern Pacific went into receivership.

The failure of the Northern Pacific also involved another line, known as the St Paul and Pacific. A relic of the heady days of the 1850s, when numerous lines in the north-west had been promoted but not built (total mileage in Minnesota in 1865 was ten), the St Paul and Pacific ran from St Paul and Minneapolis (then still known as St Anthony) for about 200 miles to Breckenridge (largely deserted since the Sioux massacre of 1862), which at high water was the head of navigation on the Red River (the Red River, like the Nile but remarkably few others, flows due north). It also had a branch line running north from St Paul along the Upper Mississippi valley to what is now Sauk Rapids, gesturing optimistically at a future junction with the Northern Pacific at Brainerd.

Unlike most other early railroad companies in Minnesota, the St Paul and Pacific had at least laid some track, but it was regarded as rather a joke, and its pretentious title did not help matters: it looked as likely to reach the Pacific as to reach the moon. Its construction in the early 1870s was financed chiefly through bonds sold in Amsterdam, but the Dutch bondholders soon grew disillusioned with their investment. Like other holders of railroad bonds, they were the victims of proprietors whose ambition was not directed towards a prosperous working railroad but was centred on the land grants and subsidies that accompanied its charter; less than half of the money subscribed for construction was actually spent to that purpose.

In order to facilitate profitable stock operations, another company was formed in 1865 called the 'First Division' of the St Paul and Pacific. This consisted of the holders of certain special and preferred stock, of whom the most substantial holder was E. B. Lichfield of Brooklyn, New York. The First Division took over the lines to Breckenridge and Sauk Rapids (then unbuilt) which, if only by virtue of their land grants in a region which was already being settled, were the most valuable attributes of the St Paul and Pacific. If the actual accomplishment of the company was absurdly small, its potential was considerably greater; by its charter, the St Paul and Pacific was authorized to construct nearly 800 miles of track, which would bring five million acres in land grants.

It was obvious that the future interests of the St Paul and Pacific and the Northern Pacific were at odds, and no less obvious that, in the contest between them, it was the latter which had the whip hand. In the course of the next few years, in fact, the Northern Pacific acquired a dominant interest in the St Paul and Pacific, which it envisaged, perhaps short-sightedly, as providing merely a feeder system for its own line. However, long before the crash of 1873 the St Paul and Pacific was tottering on the brink of collapse. With no money to further construction and small return from its operating sections (its earnings for the month of July 1873 amounted to a grand total of $305.83), the railroad was in dire straits and the final blow came when the Northern Pacific itself collapsed. This meant it was compelled to relinquish control of the St Paul and Pacific because it was unable to fulfil the conditions of its purchase of First Division stock. It was this situation, however, which gave Hill and his friends their opportunity.

To most people, the St Paul and Pacific appeared a totally worthless proposition, but one or two thought differently. In Manitoba, the country around Winnipeg was beginning to fill up with settlers, and this area urgently required a railroad link to the east. Because of the brutal nature of the country north and north-west of Lake Superior, the most obvious link was via the Red River valley and St Paul. The Red River region was still virtually uninhabited, but the observant James J. Hill had noticed there how the wheels of a wagon threw up rich, black earth, and the grass grew richly the following season in the turned-over soil of the wagon ruts.

There is some dispute as to whether the idea of taking over the St Paul and Pacific belonged originally to Hill or to Donald A. Smith (later Lord Strathcona), but it is certain that both men were considering such a scheme long before they put it into effect.

Smith, a 'strong and able man', as Hill later described him, was born in Scotland in 1820. He had come to Canada at the age of eighteen to take over a large territory on behalf of the Hudson's Bay Company, and for some years he was the uncrowned king of a vast area of harsh and rugged country. By 1870, when Hill (who had met him once before) encountered him in a snow-storm on his way down the Red River valley by dog sledge, he was a figure of considerable importance in Canada, Chief Commissioner of the Hudson's Bay Company and a member of the Dominion parliament. He had also been involved in revealing the scandal associated with the first, abortive project to build a trans-Canadian railroad.

At this and subsequent meetings, Hill and Smith agreed on the need for better north-south communications in the Red River valley. In 1874, Smith told Hill that the disillusioned Dutch bondholders of the St Paul and Pacific had approached the Hudson's Bay Company with the suggestion – swiftly rejected – that it might like to take over the bonds.

The 'associates' who eventually succeeded in taking over

167

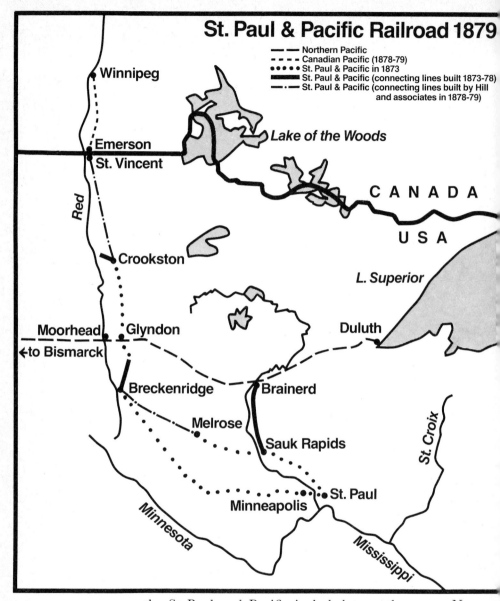

St. Paul & Pacific Railroad 1879

- — — Northern Pacific
- – – – Canadian Pacific (1878-79)
- •••• St. Paul & Pacific in 1873
- ▬▬▬ St. Paul & Pacific (connecting lines built 1873-78)
- —·—· St. Paul & Pacific (connecting lines built by Hill and associates in 1878-79)

Winnipeg

Emerson
St. Vincent

Lake of the Woods

Red

C A N A D A

U S A

Crookston

L. Superior

Moorhead Glyndon

←to Bismarck

Duluth

Breckenridge   Brainerd

Melrose

St. Croix

Sauk Rapids

Minneapolis   St. Paul

Minnesota

Mississippi

the St Paul and Pacific included two other men. Norman Kittson, was, like Smith, considerably older than Hill, and was the latter's partner in the steamboat business on the Red River. An old north-western hand, he was a considerable character in St Paul. George Stephen, another Canadian, was born in Scotland, the son of a carpenter. A shrewd and successful businessman, in the 1870s he became president of the powerful

Bank of Montreal (and later Lord Mount Stephen).

A fifth figure, who was to prove crucial to the success of the operation, was the New York banker, John S. Kennedy. He is now but dimly remembered, partly because he retired young and partly because he was never involved in any of the great financial scandals of the era, and so escaped the label of 'robber baron'. Nevertheless, when he died his estate is said to have been considerably larger than that of J. P. Morgan. Kennedy represented the interests of the Dutchmen who held the majority of the St Paul and Pacific bonds, and it was these bonds which were the crucial element in the takeover of the railroad. Having acquired the bonds, it would be possible to foreclose on the mortgages that secured them. The actual stock was regarded as worthless, and might be acquired, it was thought (rather hopefully as things turned out), without much difficulty.

Hill and Kittson, Smith and Stephen, were all men of some substance, but, of course, none of them commanded a fraction of the resources necessary to buy up the railroad. By comparison with later transactions, this was a small, though highly complex business, but it repays detailed examination both because it illustrates Hill's qualities of imagination, determination and reasoned optimism, and because it was the operation from which the whole of his career as a railroad magnate logically developed. At the time when he was devoting his extraordinary energy to the acquisition of the St Paul and Pacific (not to mention his other interests), it is doubtful how far ahead his vision extended. Certainly he was thinking of something more than through routes from St Paul to Winnipeg and Lake Superior. As a youth he had been half-obsessed with the idea of a commercial career in the Far East, and had even worked out on what stretch of the Ganges a steamboat line might most profitably be started. Since his plans for the St Paul and Pacific would inevitably involve conflict with the Northern Pacific, it is not improbable that in the early 1870s he was already dreaming of his own railroad link with the Pacific – a 'land bridge' which would fulfil the hopes of Columbus by bringing Asia to Europe's doorstep.

The Dutch bondholders were also aware that the St Paul and Pacific, despite its scrappy state of construction and its numerous debts, had some potential, but they had already been called upon for more money to keep the railroad going and were now inclined to blame themselves for throwing good money after bad. Between 1873 and 1876 various schemes were aired by different parties, including an attempt to reorganize the road in the interests of the Dutch bondholders, which foundered; meanwhile, Hill made himself familiar with every aspect of the complicated condition of the railroad, as far as he was able. In 1876 an act was passed making it possible for debtors to foreclose on a land-grant railroad without forfeiting certain benefits of the land grant, as had hitherto been the case. This had the effect of making it easier to raise capital, as railroad investors were interested not in the earning potential of the railroad (which was what interested Hill and his friends) but the security that land alone provided. At the same time, increasing immigration to the north-west and resulting increase in traffic made the St Paul and Pacific appear slightly less of a hopeless proposition. Also, the Northern Pacific had been reorganized and was showing signs of – to Hill – unwelcome revival. Two other companies, the Chicago and Northwestern and the Chicago, Milwaukee and St Paul, were also showing undesirable interest in the St Paul and Pacific. All in all, it was clear that if Hill and his associates were to succeed, they would have to be quick about it.

The first step was to find out the price at which the Dutch bondholders would be prepared to sell. Stephen thought he might be able to raise capital in London to buy the bonds, while tentative inquiries were made through Kennedy as to the Dutchmen's selling price. But 'all this', as Joseph G. Pyle wrote, 'was still subject to a thousand contingencies, and menaced by a thousand probabilities of complete breakdown. It was an agreement to divide the estate of a bankrupt individual, very ill indeed, but not yet dead, whose property was encumbered to many times its selling value [the total liabilities of the St Paul and Pacific eventually turned out to be more than $40 million, which, had he known it earlier, might have dampened even Hill's enthusiasm], about whom were flocking all the vultures of the law, and whose testamentary ideas and residuary legatees might upset the most carefully matured plans by any one of a host of unforeseeable events. It was like apportioning the winnings of tomorrow evening's play with outsiders.'

The first proposal in writing to the Dutch bondholders was made in January 1877. It was intended to divert them from their own plan of reorganization – a non-starter anyway – and its terms were less than generous. No one expected it to be accepted, but Kennedy (whose activities would nowadays lay him open to a charge of conflict of interest) welcomed this ranging shot, which at least alerted the Dutch to the possibility that the bonds might be sold, and revealed during discussions the approximate price for which the Dutch might consider selling – the information the associates were after.

On this basis the associates made a second, more concrete proposition to the Dutch in May. The letter had to be phrased rather carefully as the associates did not yet have the cash to back up their offer. Thus, what the Dutch took – and were intended to take – as a firm cash offer was so worded that the associates would be able to claim that it was merely a request for an option to buy. Much complicated bargaining ensued. The Dutch offered elaborate counter-proposals, to which the associates made further reply: one interesting feature of the documents is that the associates – or rather Hill – obviously knew much more about the railroad than did the bondholders and their representatives.

Hill usually worked at his office in St Paul until midnight, an oil lamp casting a mellow pool of light over his big rolltop desk. Once his wife, deprived of his company at home, decided to come with him in the evening. He put her in a chair by the window with a book. She fell asleep, and at 2 am he woke her and took her home.

According to Hill's calculations, the bonds were worth about $4.3 million, and this was backed up with a very precise summary of the state of the property. Something Hill did not reveal to the Dutch was that a substantial sum recently spent on improvements to the property had been charged to operating expenses. If this item were placed where it belonged, in the capital account, the railroad would have appeared rather more profitable than it did. Something else that Hill kept to himself was his own list of real and potential assets of the company which, if the bondholders had seen it, would certainly have blown the impending deal sky-high. Allowing for the completion of construction then underway, taking into account a mass of other details of which he alone was master, and estimating future earnings at what he correctly believed to be a conservative figure, Hill reckoned the value of the company at not far short of $20 million – about four times as much as the associates were offering.

Hill had fobbed off the two Chicago lines interested in the St Paul and Pacific by promising each one that the other would have no part in the operation. But in October signs of trouble from the Northern Pacific appeared when it was learned that the company was negotiating with the Canadian government to take over the (unbuilt) line from Winnipeg to the border. This would have put the St Paul and Pacific's greatest potential asset – the route to Manitoba – largely at the mercy of its bigger rival. It did, however, encourage Kennedy to recommend to the Dutch bondholders speedy acceptance of the associates' offer.

The Dutch were slowly coming round when a severe setback occurred to the associates' plans. Stephen returned from London having failed to raise the required capital; there was now no prospect that the associates could buy the bonds for cash. However, this setback had the paradoxical, though understandable, result of making the Dutch suddenly very eager to sell. They were now willing to entertain the idea of exchanging their bonds for new bonds in a company reorganized by the associates – an arrangement they would not have considered a few months earlier. Hill worked out the new agreement in January 1878. The price for the bonds remained unchanged. It was agreed to pay seven per cent interest on the purchase money until the mortgages could be foreclosed, giving the associates clear title to the property. Within six months of that date, the full price should be paid in six per cent bonds of the new company, together with a bonus of six per cent preferred stock ($250 for each $1,000 of bonds). As assurance of good intent, the associates also lodged a sum in gold with Kennedy as trustee for the Dutch. Disregarding the future profits, which not even Hill could be certain of, it was not a bad bargain for the bondholders.

Curiously, it was only at this late stage that the four associates drew up a formal agreement among themselves. 'Having full confidence in each other', as Hill's draft put it (and the confidence was justified – the four never fell out), 'and in the success of the said enterprise', they agreed that the profits (or losses) should be divided into fifths, each man receiving one-fifth plus one-fifth left for Stephen to employ in raising credit (it appears that most of this went to Kennedy).

In March 1878 the associates finally acquired the bonds – assuming they could keep to the terms of the agreement. Their immediate cash outlay was only $280,000; nevertheless, raising this comparatively small sum had stretched their personal resources to the limit. Subsequent failure would have meant ruin for Hill and Kittson, and probably also for the two Canadians. In fact, they soon became millionaires, and naturally they were to be criticized for paying the bondholders far less than the property was worth. They were in a similar situation to that of a man who buys an old painting cheaply, produces proof that it is an old master, and resells it for a fortune. The fact remains that the bondholders were keen to sell and could not have obtained a better price elsewhere at the time (the price on the New York Stock Exchange in September 1877 was about half what the associates paid). Moreover, unlike a picture dealer, the associates faced a year and a half of hard work, manifold difficulties and extreme anxiety before they saw their dreams coming true. The years 1878–79 were probably the toughest of Hill's life.

Besides their obligations to the Dutch bondholders, the associates had to find the money for the – comparatively few – bonds held elsewhere, which they purchased in the open market. They had to raise capital to complete the St Paul and Pacific line to the Canadian border. They had to refund money recently paid by the bondholders for construction of the line north of Breckenridge. They had to buy out the Litchfield stock in the company. And they had to keep the railroad, still managed by the receiver, in operation. They had problems, too numerous to list, connected with disputed land grants, recalcitrant legislatures, unpaid contractors, ownership of plant, public scepticism and public hostility. Although Stephen had not been successful in raising the $4.3 million in London, he was still president of the Bank of Montreal and the credit extended by his bank (and by Kennedy's) kept Hill and his friends above water. But some fairly desperate manoeuvres were necessary to keep things moving; at one moment Hill and Kittson raided the treasury of their Red River steamboat company for $75,000 to meet liabilities in Montreal.

*Wall Street in the late
19th century*

The immediate priority was to complete, at an estimated cost of $1 million, the unfinished lines. The line west of Melrose had to be operating by December or the land grant would be forfeited. The line to the Canadian border was less urgent so far as the land grant was concerned, but the associates' plans depended heavily on the swift completion of the link with Winnipeg (which included the Canadian track from Winnipeg south) in order, first, to check the schemes of the Northern Pacific (which did indeed build a rival line later on the other side of the Red River) and, second, to increase earnings.

Getting the Canadian connection to Winnipeg built proved a severe trial, as the Canadian government showed no inclination to meet the agreed deadline of the end of December. Hill put on what pressure he could, and went out of his way to alleviate the Canadian contractors' real or imagined difficulties by decisive action. In response to their claim, for example, that a lack of flat cars was slowing down the rate of construction, he promptly bought fifteen and had them all sent to the border. At his request, Smith arranged for an American locomotive to enter Canada to help with the track laying, and, when a small stream presented an obstruction, Hill hired a firm of St Paul builders, sketched the bridge he wanted, stood by while they built it, and sent it up north on a flat car. When the Red River pilots, crucial in transporting construction materials, struck for higher wages, Hill immediately fired them; they did not know he had men standing by to replace them.

One of the most trying problems was that, as yet, the associates were only nominally in control of the company, which was still being managed on behalf of the courts by J. P. Farley, the receiver. Farley was later to launch a long-running law suit against Hill and his friends, claiming that they had stolen his ideas and cut him out of the business (he lost the case, though the final judgement was not delivered until after Farley's death). Meanwhile, relations were friendly and co-operative, yet Farley, shrewd though barely literate, tended to move at what seemed to the exasperated Hill the pace of a paralytic tortoise, and the courts adopted a cautious attitude to the associates' plans.

Some of Farley's employees were less than satisfactory. To

Stephen, Hill complained of 'one of Mr Farley's favourites, who had full charge north of Crookston and who spent half his time in Crookston with a strumpet, and took her on the road with him on the engine, or at times would take the engine off the work in the middle of the afternoon to run down to Crookston in order that he could keep some of the other employees out of his preserve . . .'[6]

Somehow or other, the required lines were built, though they were not of the quality that Hill would demand later – shortage of iron rails was but one of Hill's day-to-day problems – and the land grants were saved. On one stretch, forfeiture of the land grant was avoided by completion of the track just twenty-four hours before the final deadline. However, this success brought attendant dangers. The completed branch line was likely to show a profit almost immediately, and would therefore be able to pay the interest on bonds before the mortgages could be foreclosed. In that case the stockholders would resume their right of control, which would result in the associates being shut out, and the value of the remainder of the property would be much reduced. Of course, the associates could have made a substantial profit on their deal with the Dutch bondholders, but that was not their purpose. They were not speculators and stock-jobbers, they were railroad men.

Hill's aggressive tactics blocked the Northern Pacific. Disregarding the fears of Stephen that a disastrous rates war might be provoked, he believed that the Northern Pacific's threats to build competing lines were mostly bluff. 'If they had any money to spare', he told Stephen, 'they would be more apt to build west of Bismarck and save their land grant.' To the Northern Pacific's proposal to build a competing line to Manitoba, Hill replied with a counter-threat to build to the west, and to ask Congress for half the Northern Pacific's land grant. This would surely have been interpreted as an empty boast if it had not been for the detailed knowledge Hill displayed of how such a line might be built. The position of the Northern Pacific was further weakened by rumours that Jay Gould, who had recently gained apparent control of the Union Pacific, had an eye on the Northern Pacific as well. Whatever the directors of the Northern Pacific believed, they decided that it was not in their interests to get into a fight with

Hill, and a mutually agreeable settlement of their claims was worked out in November 1878.

'We succeeded', Hill was to say later, 'because the time was ripe.' It would be absurd to say that Hill's timing was always fortuitous, but he did have his fair share of luck. He could hardly have calculated, for example, that the locusts would disappear from the wheat fields for good in 1877, resulting in far larger crops than had been harvested in the past.

In January 1879, the Red River line was complete and the Canadian government, after some pressure by Stephen, agreed to lease the Canadian section to the associates. Hill was already contemplating further extensions north-west from the Red River, where the richness of the country promised a flow of future settlers and the Northern Pacific might build competing lines – their truce would not last for ever. But a more pressing matter was the purchase of the Litchfield stock, which could be the cause of severe trouble if it should find its way into Northern Pacific hands. The purchase was finally accomplished by Stephen, not without difficulty. The 'old rat', as the associates were wont to refer to Litchfield, finally settled for half a million dollars. Hill thought him a robber but acknowledged, on hearing that the purchase had been agreed, 'this is the happiest news I have received for many a day'.

In March 1879, decrees for foreclosure on the mortgages were applied for and, since all stock and bondholders in the old company had been satisfied, these were speedily granted. The St Paul and Pacific was reorganized as the St Paul, Minneapolis and Manitoba Railroad Company, with Stephen as president, Hill as secretary, member of the three-man executive committee, and general manager. Total mileage of the railroad at that time was 667, of which 100 miles were under construction. Within four years, the total had more than doubled, while passenger-miles tripled and freight-miles quadrupled. Hill knew that a railroad could not stand still. It was constantly necessary to improve and expand, to seize new opportunities and to prevent rival companies cutting in. He showed foresight in acquiring a large area of land in St Paul for a terminal, big enough, as he significantly remarked, for a railroad 2,000 miles long, where other railroads eagerly rented space.

Unlike English railway companies, which were expected to

evote their profits to dividends, American railroads, as long
s they paid a steady six per cent or so, had a comparatively free
and with their surplus earnings which, in the case of the
Manitoba Railroad, could be ploughed back in the form of
mprovements (or, in other companies, creamed off in various
rays by the directors). Hill had estimated that operating
evenue would exceed costs on the Manitoba road by about
ifty per cent, and in fact this proved a conservative estimate.
Between 1879 and 1884 the Manitoba road ploughed back
bout $4 million in net profits, and this was the official figure –
he actual amount was much larger. Since high profitability
nevitably invoked criticism, demands for lower rates and so
n, Hill concealed the true profits of the company. This may
ave been dubious practice, but the concealed profits did not
o into the pockets of the directors (in 1882 Hill remarked that
ie had quite enough money and did not need to make more).
t went into the railroad.

The incident in Hill's career as a railroad magnate that
aused most controversy, and resulted in his inclusion by some
vriters in the ranks of the 'robber barons', was the issue by the
Manitoba Company in 1883 of $50 million of bonds. The
urpose was to redeem earlier bond issues and to provide an
xtra $20 million for construction, but on the surface it looked
ike a classic piece of stock watering. The company's
uthorized capital stock of $20 million was fully subscribed,
nd to increase the authorized total would have involved
egal difficulties; hence the bonds. It was proposed that the
tockholders, that is, mainly the associates, should buy the
onds, at a ratio of 1 : 2 of their stock holdings, for the price of
en cents in the dollar. The stockholders thus acquired some
10 million of securities for just $1 million.

Hill's justification was simple enough. Profits previously
pent on improvements which might otherwise have been
listributed to the stockholders amounted to $13 million, and it
vas only right and natural that the stockholders should expect
ome return for this. Since the total involved in the 'bond
;rab', as the critics called it, was only $9 million, no just cause
or criticism existed. However, his argument did not cut much
ce with the increasingly vociferous opponents of big business.

Hill's railroad business made him a very rich man, though his
esources (amounting to $50 million, with the aid of inflation,

Construction crews on the St. Paul, Minneapolis and Manitoba Railroad in Dakota Territory during the 1880s

a few years before his death) were tied up and his personal liquidity was comparatively restricted, so that he occasionally answered suggestions for personal expenditure of one kind or another by saying that he did not have the money – always an odd-sounding response from a multimillionaire, but not untruthful in this case. His fortune, moreover, was legitimate, and not the result of stock manipulation. 'If [anyone] says that Lord Strathcona or Lord Mount Stephen or Jim Hill ever made a dollar in any but an honourable and unquestionable way,' said William C. van Horne, general manager of the Canadian Pacific with whom Hill maintained a long love-hate relationship, in 1907, 'he is a damned liar.' The associates maintained a sizeable fund in New York for the sole purpose of defeating bearish raids on the St Paul, Minneapolis and Manitoba, and made their railroad a blue-chip concern. Dividends were regularly maintained, and the value of the stock remained constantly well above par.

George Stephen was also instrumental in reviving the Canadian Pacific railroad project. Canadians were eager for their own trans-continental railroad, for reasons not only of prestige, but to unite the east and west of the country. The government of John A. Macdonald insisted on an all-Canadian route, which meant crossing the uninhabited and exceedingly difficult region north of Lake Superior, a region of bogs and impervious granite. Stephen accepted this route reluctantly, but Hill, who was drawn into the project by Stephen, fought against it. As he explained later, 'the only reason for going into the Canadian Pacific scheme was for the purpose of benefiting the Manitoba road', and he argued that it made more sense for the Canadians (and more business for him) if traffic east of Winnipeg travelled through St Paul. The revivified Northern Pacific was pushing towards the west coast, and Hill knew that if his railroad was to share in the west-coast traffic, he needed the connection which the Canadian Pacific would provide.

Hill played a much less active part in building the Canadian Pacific than he had in the Manitoba railroad. Van Horne, a powerful character not unlike Hill himself, was hired as general manager, and for a time the two men co-operated well together. But it was clear to Hill that in adopting the northern route east of Winnipeg the Canadian Pacific 'assumes the position of a deadly enemy', a rival rather than a partner. It appeared that if the Manitoba railroad were to survive, it would have to have a route of its own to the Pacific. He continued active in the Canadian Pacific's interests until 1882, lending $500,000 of his stock in the Manitoba railroad as collateral for the company's short-term loans, but he felt, as his relations with the aggressive van Horne deteriorated, that his own railroad was not getting a fair deal from the Canadian Pacific. Early in 1883 he resigned, though he continued to hold a substantial quantity of Canadian Pacific stock. He had more than enough on his mind anyway – plans for the Manitoba, a new hotel, steamboats, his farm near St Paul, and his ever more frequent journeys to New York to consult with Kennedy.

A report of the Minnesota Railroad Commissioners in 1881 deplored the fact that the state's railroads were owned by outside interests. The Manitoba was the only exception, and they gloomily prophesied that it too would soon 'pass into the jaws of the anaconda which is swallowing the smaller lines as fast as it can digest and assimilate them' (their modern counterparts would put the matter less vividly).

Their forecast, however, was incorrect. Hill's line was already expanding. In the east, it gained a connection with St Cloud and Duluth, giving access to the Great Lakes traffic. In the west, the situation was more problematical; the Northern Pacific appeared to present an overpowering challenge.

The Northern Pacific had come under the control of Henry Villard (born Heinrich Hilgard), a brilliant promoter but a less capable builder or operator of railroads. In the 1870s, Villard formed the Oregon Railway and Navigation Company, which became the basis for his north-western empire. Backed by German money, he embarked upon a policy of aggressive expansion, but his methods, though sometimes brilliant, were basically unsound. One of his more remarkable coups in connection with the Oregon Railway and Navigation Company involved raising a mortgage on property which at that moment he did not own. He issued dividends almost as soon as capital was raised, the time intervening being obviously too short for the capital to be deployed in some way which made payment of dividends legitimate, and he watered stock on a scale to arouse the admiration of Jay Gould, still

spinning webs in his gloomy Fifth Avenue mansion. Villard's track along the Columbia River was cheaply built, solely to pre-empt the route and bottle up the Northern Pacific.

184

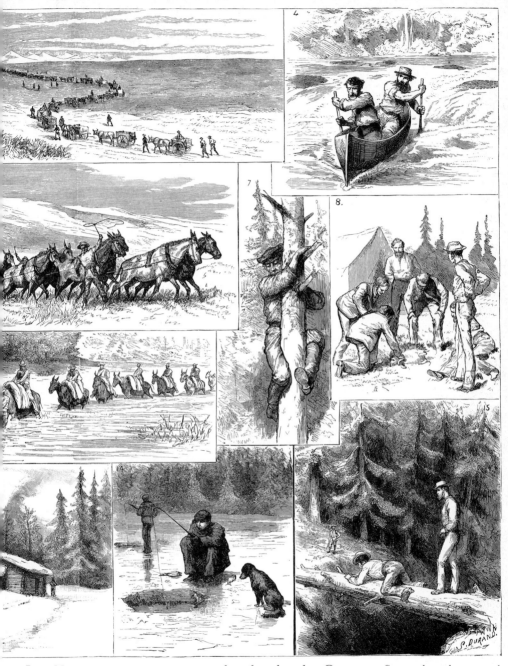

In 1880, an agreement was made whereby the Oregon Railway and Navigation Company constructed a line eastward to meet the Northern Pacific in south-east Washing-

Scenes along the proposed route of the Canadian Pacific Railroad

Henry Villard orating
triumphantly on the
completion of the
Northern Pacific line to
Gold Creek, Montana,
in 1883

BY J.E.HAYNES-ST.PAUL

ton and give it an entry to Portland, at that time the only sizeable city north of San Francisco. But meanwhile Villard was secretly acquiring as much Northern Pacific stock as he could, and in 1881 he formed his famous 'blind pool', in which his remarkable eloquence persuaded subscribers to invest the sum of $8 million without knowing for what purpose it was to be employed. This enabled him to capture a dominant interest in the Northern Pacific. Villard then formed the Oregon and Trans-continental Company, a holding company in which his Northern Pacific and Oregon Railway and Navigation interests were grouped. The same year he declared a Northern Pacific dividend of 11.1 per cent 'against improvements made from earnings'. Construction continued apace, and the transcontinental route was completed in 1883. Villard marked the event by hammering in the last, traditionally golden spike and by making a transcontinental journey by special train in less than half the time it had ever been done before.

However, construction had exceeded costs by $14 million, and this, together with other debts, created an abyss which even Villard's eloquence could not bridge – the locomotive used for the golden-spike ceremony had to be borrowed from Hill. In 1884, Villard resigned from all his enterprises, admitting that 'neither he nor the Oregon Transcontinental Company could be saved'.

Hill's system, more soundly and conservatively built, was creeping west and undercutting the Northern Pacific's rates. By 1883, the line had reached Devil's Lake, North Dakota, a second connection had been made with Winnipeg west of the Red River, all the old lines had been rebuilt in steel, and a great clearing yard for freight cars, the 'Minneapolis Transfer', had been created. Hill still took a detailed interest in the conduct of the railroad. His letters and memoranda include notes of coal stains at the Grand Forks depot, of a plank needed for repairs to a platform, and of a car repairer who 'smells of whiskey'. In his house in St Paul Hill was building up his art collection. His taste was good but conservative. He admired the Barbizon school and owned several Corots and Millets, but he turned down Daumier's *Third-Class Railway Carriage* when it was first offered to him. He bought it some years later, but he never seems to have come around to the Impressionists. Like many railroad men (and sailors), he was intensely interested in farming, and he tried to persuade the farmers of the north-west to diversify, even supplying bulls, bought from Britain, for a nominal sum to encourage stock-raising. These more or less charitable endeavours, however, failed to endear him to the farmers, who like farmers everywhere bitterly blamed the railroads not only for their rates but for any other misfortune which could somehow be attributed to them. 'After the grasshoppers', the farmers of the north-west complained, 'we had Jim Hill.'

Both the Canadian Pacific and the Northern Pacific were in and out of financial trouble, and both relied on government support of some kind. To run a third Pacific route between them without similar support seemed like madness. But Hill did it, and he did it successfully. In the 1880s, the agricultural and mineral potential of Montana was attracting keen attention, and had an effect on the plans of both the Northern Pacific and the Union Pacific. Mountainous country limited the available routes, and Federal permission was necessary in order to cross the Indian Reservations. Hill kept his plans quiet for fear of exciting competitors and frightening investors, but in 1883 he had firmly decided to build into Montana and, ultimately, through to the Pacific.

The Montana Central Railroad, between Great Falls (head of Missouri navigation) and Helena, was organized in January 1886. In effect it was entirely a Hill enterprise: what appeared to be purely local lines promoted by local interests often turned out to have been inspired by Hill as branches of his system. The main line was soon streaking westward from Devil's Lake towards a connection with the Montana Central. President Cleveland had vetoed the first bill to permit the Manitoba to build through the Indian Reservation, a shock to Hill, one of Cleveland's admirers (they later became friends and salmon-fishing companions), but a second bill was approved in 1887. Over $800,000 was spent on surveys, sometimes made in the depth of winter, in accordance with Hill's policy of low gradients and gentle curves, which allowed locomotives on his lines to haul loads far greater than the national average. The Manitoba reached Minot, named after a brilliant young lieutenant of Hill's who was killed in a train crash in 1890, in 1886 and in the following year completed the 500-mile stretch to Great Falls. On the easier stretches the rate

189

Federal permission to lay tracks across the Indian Reservations in Montana was finally granted in 1887, enabling Hill to go ahead with plans for a third Pacific route

of construction reached seven miles a day, though elsewhere
the frost was so deep that the earth had to be blasted with
dynamite. Over 8,000 men were employed, many of them
veterans of the Canadian Pacific. The railroad was called by
some people 'Hill's folly', and it paid no returns on investment
for several years. But it was built well, and its freight – at first

almost entirely wheat – was soon augmented by coal and other minerals, the mines being served by branch lines.

Having built his railroad into the Rocky Mountains, Hill was unlikely to leave it dangling at Helena or Butte, though many people still refused to believe that a Pacific connection was seriously intended. Construction through the mountains to the

The last spike is driven home in the construction of the Great Northern Railway in 1893

193

coast would take much more time and money, but there wa
no longer a pressing need for speed as the Montana traffic had
already been secured – before rivals could draw it off – and any
new railroad was likely to be welcomed on the bustling north-
west coast. In fact, Hill at this time was thinking in terms of
something far more ambitious than a connection between the
Great Lakes and the Pacific.

New rivalries and new alliances were formed constantly in
the railroad business. In 1887 Hill entered a friendly alliance
with the Chicago, Burlington and Quincy system. This
railroad, stretching like a cummerbund across the stomach of
America – the great bread basket of the mid-west – was one of
the most solidly constructed and well-run railroads in the
country (built, like Hill's line, without the aid of land grants).
In exchange for the hospitality of the Manitoba in giving it
access to the north-west, the Burlington gave Hill an excellent
route to Chicago; but the idea of the Burlington becoming
part of Hill's empire seemed, in 1887, as probable as a minnow
swallowing a whale. The following year Hill also organized
the Northern Steamship Company to link up with his vast new
terminal and dock scheme on Lake Superior, with steamers
much larger, and therefore cheaper, than any rivals, to carry
corn to Buffalo.

Railroads, like the English aristocracy, adopted rather
bewildering changes of name as they grew grander. The St
Paul and Pacific had become the St Paul, Minneapolis and
Manitoba; in 1889, it became the Great Northern Railway
Company.

In completing the final link with the Pacific coast, one
possibility to be considered was to buy rather than build.
There were plenty of lines in the north-west looking for a rich
uncle, and the passage of the Interstate Commerce Act
(1887), whatever its intentions, tended to encourage co-
operation and amalgamation. But there was no line available
which came up to Hill's standards of low operating costs. 'We
do not care enough for Rocky Mountain scenery', he wrote in
1890, 'to spend a large sum of money in developing it. . . What
we want is the best possible line, shortest distance, lowest
grades, and least curvature that we can build'. By these means
Hill made a line on which he could cut rates to a point below
actual cost on any competing railroad and still make a profit.

In December 1890 Hill was among those present at a meeting organized by J. P. Morgan to work out amicable agreements, including standard rates, on western railroads. But Hill never put much faith in such 'gentlemen's agreements'. There was already a hint of an approaching depression in the air, enough to worry the more percipient holders of stock in western railroads. The Union Pacific, with its huge debts, made tentative approaches to Hill, but he remarked that he thought it 'doubtful if anyone can get either honor or profit out of their affairs'. On the other hand, he had written to Stephen as early as May 1889 explaining the advantages to be gained from control of the Northern Pacific. Villard had made a comeback by 1889 and his Oregon and Transcontinental Company narrowly controlled the Northern Pacific, while sharing with the Union Pacific control of the Oregon Railway and Navigation Company. The Northern Pacific's line to the coast had been completed (1883) and Villard was rumoured to be after the Great Northern. That ambition was hopeless, but it confirmed Hill in his plans to make himself the supremo of the north-west.

Meanwhile, the greatest piece of railway construction for which Hill was responsible throughout his long career was under way. Three years were spent surveying the route through to the Pacific, the trickiest problem being to find a way through the mountains. The only feasible route through the Rockies seemed to be the Marias Pass. The pass then so named had been discovered in 1853–54, but it was 7,600 feet above sea level and well above the snow line – far from satisfactory for a railroad. It would require a two-and-a-half-mile tunnel just to get through at 5,450 feet. However, there were rumours of other passes, accommodating tributaries of the Marias River, and Hill was determined to find a better alternative. The man he employed was an intrepid Yankee explorer named John F. Stevens, who came up trumps when on December 11, 1889, in a temperature forty degrees below freezing, he discovered the 'real' Marias Pass at about 5,215 feet. Today his statue marks the spot, near the edge of Glacier National Park.

Work began the following spring, and the whole 900-mile length of line was soon swarming with workmen. The job, as one of Hill's assistants put it, was a 'desperate scramble'. It is said that hunters still sometimes come upon the bones of those who died from exposure during the winter of 1890–91 Stevens's survey of the Cascades (the coastal range) forced Hill to recognize that he would have to compromise his usual methods of construction, and the result was a 'switchback' zig-zag up the mountains, not replaced by the more desirable tunnel until ten years later (the present tunnel is a still later work, though forecast by Hill before his death). Hill, never an easy employer (his comments on work in progress, said one of his workmen with commendable understatement, were 'not always suave'), was busier than ever: the telegraph line buzzed with his messages and his private car, which had an unfortunate tendency to slip off the rails, trundled constantly back and forth. Hill had planned for the two sections to meet somewhere in the Cascades before the winter of 1892. For once, to his great anger, his deadline was not met, but the final spike was driven in on January 6, 1893. Less than fifteen years had passed since Hill and his associates had gained control of the puny, struggling St Paul and Pacific with its 500 miles of rusty track. It had been transformed into a mighty system spanning the continent between the Great Lakes and the Pacific Ocean.

The Great Northern opened in the first month of the year in which a major financial crash heralded a long and severe depression. As credit dried up almost totally, it was an anxious time for practically everyone – but the Great Northern survived it. The Northern Pacific, however, was among those swiftly delivered into the hands of the receivers, its bankruptcy hastened by competition with Hill's line, on which freight costs were reduced to a quarter-cent per ton-mile.

Retrenchment was required. 'Take whatever steps are necessary to reduce track, machinery, stations and other service to lowest point possible,' Hill telegraphed. 'Take off all extra gangs. . . Reduce wages. .'. There would be plenty of men available, he observed grimly, to work for lower wages. The depression coincided, however, with much-improved harvests, and, thanks to its low operating costs, the Great Northern was able to make a profit on rates which other railroads could not have sustained. By 1896 Hill was again trying to tuck away excess profits where they would not be noticed. Unfortunately for him, though, news of his success

One of the biggest problems in the building of the Great Northern was laying track over the Rocky Mountains. 'Snow sheds' had to be erected as protection against avalanches

inevitably spread, and, not surprisingly, the combination of high profits and low wages provoked strikes. Hill, having failed to reach a compromise at a meeting with the socialist leader of the American Railway Union, Eugene V. Debs, lost his temper and demanded that President Cleveland send in troops to act against the strikers. The situation was not that bad, although soon afterwards the authorities did send troops to break the Pullman Strike in Chicago. The difficulties of this period were reflected not only in a noticeable shortening of Hill's temper but also in his increased political activity, an area in which he moved clumsily, though his views on the 'free silver' question were sound; the advent of William Jennings Bryan turned him into a Republican. Hill wrote to his wife on their silver wedding anniversary that their future would be happiest 'if we are left largely to our children and ourselves', but whatever his devotion to family life, he became more and more a public figure. Mrs Hill's diary in 1901 sadly recorded: 'We see by the papers that papa is hurrying back from the coast.'

Schemes to reorganize the Northern Pacific were being aired even before it went bankrupt. The German shareholders looked to J. P. Morgan, who already had a well-established reputation as a restorer of bankrupt properties in the east, and to James J. Hill, who had shown how to operate a railroad soundly. Hill, as he had said to Stephen, was well aware of 'the advantages to our company [which] would mainly come from the freedom of competition and needless friction and expense in operation' if the Northern Pacific were taken over. After much discussion between the various interested parties, the plans for the reorganization of the Northern Pacific were agreed at a meeting in Morgan's house in London in May 1895. The crux of the deal was that the bonds of the reorganized company were to be guaranteed by the Great Northern in exchange for half its capital stock, but this monopoly of transport by Hill in the north-west encountered fierce public criticism. More importantly, an adverse judgement was passed on the scheme by the Supreme Court, after various lower courts had passed conflicting judgements on whether the plan infringed a law that 'No railroad corporation shall consolidate with, lease or purchase ... any other railroad corporation ... which owns or controls a parallel or competing line.'

This legal snag was circumvented by doing privately – and legally – what could not be done publicly: the Great Northern stockholders, acting as private individuals, bought the Northern Pacific bonds, and, in combination with Morgan's group, secured a majority. Hill himself had a substantial holding which, given the alliance with Morgan (a firm one, never broken), gave him a strong interest but not complete control. It meant that he had to go 'repeatedly through the familiar cycle of sweet reasonableness, righteous indignation and kiss-and-make-up' in order to get his way. The two railroads remained separate, and though in alliance, relations were often uneasy. Hill found the situation frustrating, and eventually Morgan came around to his view; a readjustment of executive powers towards the end of 1900 gave Hill complete working control of the Northern Pacific, and he rapidly organized a more sensible unification of the two lines. 'It makes me almost giddy', wrote Stephen, now based in England but still a close friend and associate, 'when I think of the "two streaks of rust" which we bought from the Dutchmen 21 years ago.'

In 1900, therefore, the Northern Pacific was securely in the hands of Hill and Morgan, or so it appeared. One man, however, was not so sure.

Edward H. Harriman was born in Long Island in 1848, third of six children of a somewhat feckless Episcopal minister who, soon after Harriman's birth, wandered off to California for a year. The family was poor and the boy left school at fourteen to take a job as an office junior in Wall Street, rising in the course of time to the post of chief clerk in a broker's office. At the age of twenty-one he bought a seat on the Stock Exchange with the aid of a loan from an uncle, and he was soon operating a thriving brokerage. But his ambition led him into more creative forms of money-making than bearish deals in stocks and shares, and in 1877 he made his first venture into the transport business when he bought a small Hudson River steamboat, which, however, he soon sold again at a profit – a characteristic Harriman operation. Soon afterwards he married the daughter of a banker, William J. Averell, who was also president of a small railroad company in upstate New York. Had it not been for this connection, perhaps Harriman would never have become a railroad magnate.

E. H. Harriman

As a young man, Harriman seems to have been a rather different personality from the austere, coldly calculating automaton the public visualized him as in later years. Acquaintances described him as companionable and light-hearted. Arriving for a vacation in the Adirondacks, he jumped off the stage, hunting rifle in hand, and (he was an expert marksman) promptly put a shot straight through the gilded globe on top of the flagpole in front of the hotel. That this display was not out of character is proved by the testimony of a friend who had arrived earlier at the hotel and, eyeing the seductive target, had accurately forecast Harriman's reaction. Small in build, he was a keen outdoorsman and athlete, a good boxer, and the founder in 1876 of the Tompkins Square Boys' Club on the Lower East Side of New York City, one of the earliest attempts to provide suitable recreation for the children of the urban slums.

Harriman's reputation as a rebuilder of bankrupt railroads dated from his purchase of an obscure and decrepit concern called the Lake Ontario Southern in 1881. Having bought out the old directors inexpensively, he reorganized and renamed the company, then sold it at a good profit to the Pennsylvania Railroad, a step he had, of course, been planning when he set about gaining control.

His attention then turned to bigger game. The Illinois Central was one of the oldest and most successful lines in the country, and among its most influential directors was Stuyvesant Fish, an old friend of Harriman. Fish assisted him in acquiring substantial holdings of the company's securities, which were low-priced due to scepticism about the Illinois Central's current expansion programme. Harriman also gained the confidence – and the proxies – of the Dutch investors in the line, who made up a substantial minority. In 1883, he became a director of the company and the proponent of a policy of rapid expansion. During the next five years the railroad bought or built an additional thousand miles of track. One of its acquisitions was the Dubuque and Sioux City Railroad, the occasion of Harriman's first clash with J. P. Morgan: it ended in victory for Harriman, who employed a legal manoeuvre to get Morgan's proxies rejected at the company's annual meeting.

Harriman's tactics provoked a good deal of doubt and suspicion in business circles. He was widely regarded as a financier in the mould of Jay Gould, whom in many ways he resembled, and it looked as though Harriman might do for (or to) the Illinois Central what Gould had done for the Erie. There was, however, a fundamental difference. Harriman's first big railroad deal had taught him the importance of the physical condition of the property, and whatever his financial ethics, Harriman did not ruin the railroads he ran – he improved them. The traditionally strong credit of the Illinois Central was maintained, and in the depression of the 1890s Harriman financed expansion with bonds paying only three per cent, a remarkably low price for capital. Harriman was always good at 'buying money'.

In the 1890s, Harriman was still unknown to the public at large; Wall Street knew him merely as a very successful broker, while even in railroad circles he was far from a celebrated figure, for the success of the Illinois Central had been largely credited to Fish. But Harriman was engaged in an operation which, if successful, would change all that and make his name known internationally.

The panic of 1893 which bankrupted the Northern Pacific also ruined the Union Pacific. The history of this great railroad had been chequered, to say the least. In 1880 it had taken over large new commitments, at the usual uneconomic price, largely as a result of the machinations of Jay Gould. Between 1884 and 1890 it was managed by a very different figure, Charles Francis Adams, but he too followed a policy of large-scale acquisitions which, however justifiable on other grounds, aggravated the basic problem of over-capitalization. Adams was eventually forced out by Gould, and when the Panic struck, the Union Pacific, along with 155 other railroad companies, was bound for the receivers.

A reorganization committee, which fleetingly included J. P. Morgan, was formed, but after eighteen months during which the Union Pacific lost nearly half its mileage and appeared to be falling apart, the committee resigned in despair. A new approach was then made by the holders of the dwindling Union Pacific securities to Jacob Schiff, head of the powerful banking house of Kuhn, Loeb and Company. Schiff called on Morgan to learn that the House of Morgan neither had nor wanted to have anything to do with the company and, reassured, he managed to persuade various other people, including Vanderbilt associates, to serve on a new reorganization committee. For a time his plans went well, but in 1896 he became aware of unexpected opposition. Criticism was voiced in Congress, hostile articles appeared in the press, stockholders raised inexplicable objections. Schiff was puzzled. He came to the conclusion that Morgan must be behind it all and went to see him again. Morgan repeated that he wanted nothing to do with the railroad, but said he would make some inquiries. Some time later he sent for Schiff. 'It's that little fellow Harriman,' he told him, 'and you want to look out for him.'

Schiff was astonished. He knew Harriman only slightly and could not imagine what he was up to. He arranged to meet him, and asked him frankly if he knew who was behind the opposition. 'I am the man,' Harriman admitted. 'But why are you doing it?' 'Because I intend to reorganize the Union Pacific myself.' Schiff smiled, as though addressing a ten-year-old boy who had announced his intention to be President, and inquired just how Harriman proposed to do it. He was soon enlightened. Harriman was prepared to issue $100 million in three per cent bonds of the Illinois Central, for which he expected to get very close to par value. Schiff, as he pointed out, could not get capital for less than four and a half per cent.

Somewhat chastened, Schiff asked Harriman's price. Harriman agreed to co-operate if Schiff made him chairman of the reorganizing committee. Schiff said that was impossible. 'Very well, Mr Schiff,' said Harriman, 'Go ahead and see what you can do. Good day.'

Schiff soon found that Harriman could not be ignored, and he proposed a compromise, under which Harriman would become a director and member of the executive committee, commenting 'If you prove to be the strongest man in that committee, you'll probably get the chairmanship in the end.' Schiff's financing syndicate, including Harriman, gained possession of the Union Pacific (less its numerous branch lines which had already been lost) in November 1897, and in the following year Harriman began buying Union Pacific stock, mostly at less than twenty-five per cent of par, confident that under his management the enterprise would soon prove profitable. Within nine years this investment, through dividends and rising value, was paying a profit of over sixty per cent. The revivified Union Pacific regained possession of many of the lines it had lost, including the Oregon Short Line and the Oregon Railway and Navigation Company, and in 1898 Harriman, who had gained the full confidence of Schiff, became chairman of the executive committee. Within three years the revenue of the Union Pacific was more than doubled and 'by 1901', wrote William Z. Ripley, 'the company was in prime financial condition, with strong credit and unsurpassed banking connections'.

While the work of reconstructing the line was under way Harriman took a holiday. Like everything else he did, it was on the grand scale – an expedition to Alaska and Siberia in a hired steamer, during which Harriman shot one of the great grizzlies of Kodiak Island and discovered an unknown fjord in Prince William Sound. A large group of scientists accompanied the expedition, and to one of them Harriman explained his attitude to wealth. 'I never cared for money except as power for work . . . What I most enjoy is the power of creation, getting into partnership with Nature in doing good, helping to feed man and beast, and making everybody and everything a little better and happier.' Many millionaires have adumbrated similar explanations of their activities, frequently without conscious cynicism.

By 1900 the Union Pacific was strong and healthy, but for its traffic through to the west coast it still depended on the Central Pacific, a line much inferior in construction (its curves between Ogden and Reno equalled thirty-six complete circles) and capacity, and unlikely to be improved, due to financial stringencies, by its current proprietors, the Southern Pacific. Harriman's first offers to buy the line were rejected, but, in August 1900, the picture was transformed when Collis P. Huntington, the 'father' of the Central Pacific and a major stockholder, died.

The market value of Huntington's vast Southern Pacific Company was about $100 million. If the Union Pacific was to gain control of the Southern Pacific Company it would have to spend over $50 million, rather an intimidating sum for a concern which had so recently emerged from bankruptcy. Harriman, who foresaw not only the chance to increase Union Pacific business by acquiring the Central Pacific but also a chance to eliminate competition by acquiring the Southern Pacific, was not intimidated. An issue of $100 million Union Pacific bonds at four per cent was successfully marketed: the bonds were convertible, and speculators anticipated (correctly) a future rise in Union Pacific stock. Kuhn, Loeb began buying Southern Pacific stock, but the crucial element, if control were to be gained, was the stock of the Huntington estate. Despite intense competition for this, Harriman managed to persuade Huntington's heirs to sell to him. This, with the purchases in the market, gave the Union Pacific thirty-eight per cent of the Southern Pacific's stock which, if not enough to assure outright control, was enough to prevent anyone else getting it and to give the Union Pacific interests time to build up their holdings further. Within a few months, control was total. The Southern Pacific, probably the biggest railroad network in the world, was united with the Union Pacific under Harriman's direction. It was the largest railroad amalgamation up to that time and made Harriman the greatest railroad magnate in the country. He had risen like a rocket, and showed no signs of burning out, but the next stage brought him on to a collision course with James J. Hill.

The conflict between the two railroad titans of the age arose from the somewhat complicated railroad situation in the Pacific North-West (see map p. 206). In the 1880s, Villard's strategically situated Oregon Railway and Navigation Company had provided the Northern Pacific with its link to tidewater, from Spokane to Portland (the chief significance of Portland lay in the fact that it could be reached, via the Columbia River valley, without crossing the formidable Cascades). Subsequently, both the Northern Pacific and the Great Northern had built their own tracks to Puget Sound. Meanwhile, the Union Pacific entered the area via its subsidiary, the Oregon Short Line (completed in 1881), which connected with the Oregon Railway and Navigation line to run into Portland. This connection had become necessary to the Union Pacific because of its unsatisfactory relations with the Central Pacific (Ogden–San Francisco). The Central Pacific under Collis P. Huntington had made life difficult for the Union Pacific largely because Huntington and his associates were busy with their own transcontinental, the Southern Pacific, which ran the length of California and across the south-west to New Orleans. This forced the Union Pacific into building the Oregon Short Line and diverted its main traffic from the due-west route (to San Francisco) to the north-west, and the new alignment was confirmed when Harriman gained control of the Oregon Railway and Navigation Company. The Union Pacific then became a fully developed north-west line in direct competition with the Great Northern and the Northern Pacific.

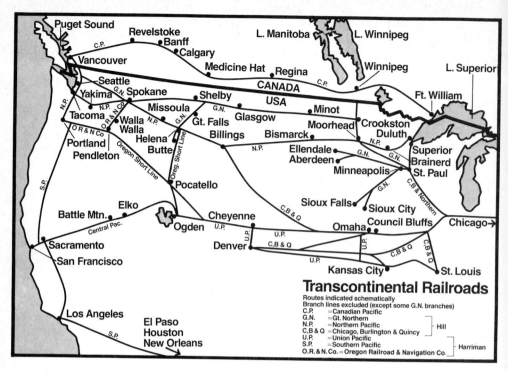

To reach the growing centres of Tacoma and Seattle, the Union Pacific needed to use the Northern Pacific line from Portland to Seattle. Of greater significance, however, was the need of the Great Northern and the Northern Pacific to use the Oregon Railway and Navigation line along the Columbia River to Portland. During the depression of the mid-1890s, the Oregon Railway and Navigation line was co-operatively shared, but the advent of Harriman, with his large ambitions, made this vital link appear increasingly fragile.

The contest between Hill and Harriman was not confined to the north-west. The events leading to the stock-market crisis of 1901 were sparked off by developments in the mid-west. Hill and Morgan agreed on the desirability of acquiring a railroad that would give their Great Northern-Northern Pacific system an independent entry to Chicago and the markets of the mid-west. There were a number of possible candidates, but the one Hill preferred was the Chicago, Burlington and Quincy, which included a line from Minneapolis to Chicago and a line running from its Nebraska heartland north-west to connect with the Northern Pacific at Billings, Montana. With nearly

8,000 miles of track the Burlington, popularly known as the 'Q', was a real 'widows-and-orphans' company, a solid blue-chip investment. However, its directors were ruefully aware that, unless they had a line to the Pacific, their future would be one of dwindling earnings.

Morgan's eastern interests led him to favour the takeover of another company, the Chicago, Milwaukee and St Paul, and there was a third alternative, the Wisconsin Central, once controlled by the Northern Pacific but reorganized as an independent company after the Northern Pacific bankruptcy in the 1890s. This line was ruled out on the grounds of its poor physical condition and relatively indirect route, and when Morgan failed to persuade the Chicago, Milwaukee and St Paul – part-owned by Rockefeller interests inimicable to Morgan – to sell, Hill's original choice became the objective. 'The Burlington', as Albro Martin put it, 'was the most eligible belle in the West, and she did not want for suitors.' The Boston men who still largely controlled the company saw that they must sell, but they were determined to get a high price for their stockholders – $200 cash per share, well above market price.

A glance at the map shows the obvious advantages to the Northern Pacific of the Burlington lines, especially the line from Billings; it shows also how the Burlington system was of hardly less significance to the Union Pacific, which offered an alternative connection to the Pacific North-West via the Oregon Short Line. However, perhaps the decisive motive for both the Hill and Harriman interests in their pursuit of the Burlington belle was to prevent the other side getting hold of her. Certainly, if Harriman gained control of the system, he would have neatly fenced off the Hill lines from the important, growing markets of the mid-west and south. If Hill gained control, there was a danger that he might extend the Burlington from Denver to the Pacific in direct competition with the Union Pacific.

Such a development was never part of Hill's plans, but Harriman could not be certain of that. His suspicions were to be further aroused early in 1901 by a local railroad being built from the Utah copper mines to Los Angeles, which looked as though it might turn out to be the final section of a Burlington extension from Denver. Taking advantage of an old right-of-way, Harriman hastily despatched his own construction gang to build a parallel line. It soon appeared that the main purpose was not to construct but to obstruct, and the two gangs spent more time fighting each other than they did in laying track.

Meanwhile, Harriman made an offer for the Burlington which was rejected; he was taken aback when Charles E. Perkins, president of the Burlington, told him the price was $200 a share. Jacob Schiff, of the bankers Kuhn, Loeb, began quietly buying Burlington stock on the open market, but there was no hope of obtaining control that way. Harriman apparently thought the asking price was too high; at any rate, he never made an offer close enough to the figure required for Perkins to consider it. Moreover Perkins, though he naturally put his company's stockholders first, regarded the Hill-Morgan group as the preferable purchaser.

Hill also thought the price was high, but, unlike Harriman, he believed the property was worth it. He remarked to Stephen that the price might seem excessive at the moment, but in a few years' time it would look like a bargain. The deal, in which the Great Northern and the Northern Pacific divided the Burlington equally between them, was finally concluded against the background of the approaching stock market panic brought about by Harriman's alternative strategy, which brings us back to the situation in the north-west, a situation which Joseph G. Pyle compared with the state of the Balkans in Europe in 1914.

Harriman's bold plan, activated by the Hill-Morgan acquisition of the Burlington, was to take over the Northern Pacific. He was supported by Schiff of Kuhn, Loeb – roughly equivalent to the alliance of Morgan with Hill – and by Standard Oil-Rockefeller money, but on both sides various individuals – some appearing in more than one role – and organizations were involved, so that to speak of the contestants as 'Hill' and 'Harriman' is to some extent a convenient piece of shorthand. These two powers, with no other significant challengers, divided the railroads west of the Mississippi between them, Hill representing the 'North' (the Great Northern and the Northern Pacific) and Harriman the 'South' (the Union Pacific and the Southern Pacific). The battle of 1901 was fought to decide which of these two should reign supreme.

Harriman always maintained, rightly or wrongly, that the

Burlington had been acquired by his rivals in an underhand way, though Hill insisted that he had kept him informed that negotiations were under way. Harriman accordingly demanded that the Union Pacific should have an equal share in the Burlington with the Great Northern and the Northern Pacific, offering to pay one-third of the purchase price. He was told it was too late and that anyway such an arrangement would be illegal under the law forbidding the union of competing railroads. Some moderately unfriendly remarks were made on either side, Schiff for instance referring to profits made 'by the friends of Mr Hill' through deals in Burlington stock during the negotiations for purchase. Hill, anxious to avoid a row, argued, not very convincingly, that Hill-Morgan ownership of the Burlington was in the best interests of the Union Pacific since the Burlington would no longer be tempted to build its own line to the West Coast duplicating the Union Pacific's, a statement which, as we have seen, Harriman regarded as unreliable.

Harriman now decided, as one writer put it, that if he could not get the filly he would buy the mare. It was a spirited decision on the part of 'the little man'. Villard had once captured the Northern Pacific for $8 million; the sum now required was nearly ten times as much. However, since the Hill-Morgan allies owned much less than fifty per cent of Northern Pacific stock, Harriman's effort to gain control was in theory at least perfectly feasible. Hill and Morgan had never considered the possibility seriously. Nor had anyone else, except Harriman.

Backed by Rockefeller money and by New York bankers like James Stillman eager to topple Morgan from his eminence, Harriman did not lack resources. His immediate problem was to acquire Northern Pacific stock without alerting the market to the fact that he was the purchaser. He started buying in April, and Hill soon realized that someone was 'throwing stones into my yard', as he put it, but before the cat was let out of the bag the damage had been done. One unsuspecting stockholder sold $3.5 million the day before a telegram arrived from Hill asking him not to – a request he would have granted if received in time. As late as May 2, Morgan's company sold $1 million of Northern Pacific, presumably not realizing where it was going. Hill was furious when he heard of it; Morgan, most inconveniently, was in Europe, keeping company with an aristocratic French lady according to gossip. Hill had arrived in New York himself on May 1, and watched askance as the price of Northern Pacific stock rose steadily. On May 2 Harriman had apparently succeeded in his object: the following day Schiff advised Hill that the Harriman interests now held control of the Northern Pacific. They had acquired $78 million of the stock, a clear though narrow majority of the total of $155 million.

Harriman offered to put Hill in charge of the combined properties, including the Union Pacific and the Southern Pacific. 'You are the boss', he said. 'We are all working for you. Give me your orders.' This was a handsome bribe indeed, but there was no chance of Hill throwing over Morgan, to whom he immediately wired an account of the situation.

Harriman's control of the Northern Pacific was not, in fact, so secure as it appeared on the surface. The Northern Pacific stock was made up of common and preferred shares, and Harriman's acquisitions included a majority of the preferred stock but not of the common stock. Both kinds carried voting rights, so Harriman, with his overall majority, was in a position to elect his own board of directors at the annual meeting due in October. However, the ultimate control of the company lay with the holders of the common stock. They had the power to retire the preferred stock (that is, to call in the certificates in exchange for cash payment at par value) on the first day of any year. Since October comes before January, Harriman's board of directors would be in control and could prevent this happening. But there was one further consideration – the clincher as it turned out. The current Hill-Morgan directors had the power to postpone the company's annual meeting until the New Year. They could thus prolong their own tenure until January 1 came around, when the preferred stock could be retired, annihilating Harriman's majority. (None of these things could be done quite as easily as they can be stated; for example, to retire the preferred stock would require a cash outlay of $75 million.)

However, the battle was not yet lost or won, because the Hill-Morgan interests did not own a majority of the common stock either. Out of a total of $80 million, Harriman held

perhaps $37 million and Hill-Morgan a maximum of $28 million. By buying the outstanding $15 million of common stock, Hill and Morgan could ensure impregnable control. This was a tough decision to make. The market was already inflated and feverish; further purchases would send prices soaring; all kinds of speculative deals would be made, causing great confusion; old friends, tempted by enormous profits, might prove unreliable. In fact, no one could say what might happen. On Saturday, May 4, Morgan telegraphed from Aix-les-Bains approving Hill's recommendation that they should

Hill's, Morgan's and Harriman's attempts at consolidation of railroads were temporarily blocked by the governor of Minnesota; later, the Federal government proved an unbeatable opponent

211

buy 150,000 shares of Northern Pacific common stock. On Monday morning, when the stock market opened, Morgan's brokers began to buy. In no time the market was virtually swept bare of Northern Pacific stock. The price leapt upwards seventeen and a half points and total trading in Northern Pacific totalled $35 million in the one day. Hill told the Press, untruthfully, that he did not know what was going on, and the general impression was that Harriman had cornered him (Harriman himself was not quite certain). Panic reigned on Wall Street. On May 9 Northern Pacific was quoted at the ludicrous figure of $1,000, while all other stocks sank like a stone. It was, wrote Morgan's biographer Carl Hovey, 'a curious and terrible state of affairs ...; the extraordinary need for cash, for four or five days, had steadily forced the sale of all kinds of stock except "N.P.", and now the selling movement suddenly became a deluge which swept all values madly downward. So many shares were sold that it was impossible to keep track of them all, while above this ghastly confusion and wreckage, balloon high, hung the perfidious cause of it all – the stock which no one could buy.'

Meanwhile, Hill knew, and Morgan in his French resort knew also, that the Northern Pacific had been saved. Harriman had shown boldness and imagination, but he had missed the boat by not ensuring that he had a majority of the common stock before he struck. It appears that he had intended to make it impossible for Morgan to buy the vital 150,000 shares, but his plans had gone awry partly because he was ill at home during the weekend of May 4–5. When, on Saturday, he gave the order for Kuhn, Loeb to buy, Schiff was at the synagogue; he did not receive the message immediately, and when he did receive it, he advised against buying further. He had no contact with Harriman until some time after the market had opened on Monday morning (telephones had been in use for over twenty years and the lack of communication at this vital moment is curious), and, by the time Harriman discovered his order to buy had not been carried out, the purchases by Morgan's brokers had driven the price of the stock so high that it was impossible to carry out the scheme successfully.

The fact remained that the Harriman group held an overall majority of Northern Pacific stock. If the battle had been fought to a finish it would have been a bloody and bitter one, the result uncertain except that there could have been no true winner. Both parties realized that compromise was essential. In the financial frenzy a large quantity of Northern Pacific stock had been sold 'short', and many people would have been ruined if contracts had been pressed.

The compromise finally arrived at took the form of a gigantic holding company called the Northern Securities Company, chartered in New Jersey in November 1901. Its capital of $400 million (beyond the reach of even a raider as bold as Harriman) was issued to acquire most of the capital stock of the Northern Pacific and the Great Northern (which together, of course, owned the Burlington), which came under the joint control of the Hill and Harriman groups. Hill had considered such a solution long before the Harriman raid. Harriman, owning twenty-three per cent of the stock (mainly the fruit of his Northern Pacific purchases), had a seat on the board and so did two of his associates, including Schiff. The other twelve directors represented the Hill-Morgan group. Hill was elected president.

Setting up the Northern Securities Company was, said Hill, 'the hardest job I have ever undertaken', but an important question remained: was it legal? Trust-busting was becoming fashionable, and the announcement of the creation of the vast Northern Securities Company was followed by an outburst of public hostility which grew steadily louder. Their lawyers had advised Hill and Morgan that the new corporation, being merely an investment company which, though it held the securities of the two railroads, played no part in operating them, would not infringe the Sherman Anti-Trust Act of 1890. Unfortunately, a lawyers' opinion, no matter how expensive, is only an opinion, and often subject to rude shocks in the courts. Moreover, the lawyers failed to take political considerations into account. Theodore Roosevelt, having recently reached the White House through President McKinley's assassination, was looking for popular causes. The Northern Securities Company offered one. In February 1902 the Federal government brought a suit against the company, inaugurating one of the most famous cases in American business history. Though some of his associates were prepared to back down, Hill, who rightly regarded the company as his baby, fought hard to establish its legality. The final judgement was delivered – inevitably – in the Supreme Court in March 1904. The justices voted five to four in favour of dissolution of the company. The powerful dissenting opinion of Justice Oliver Wendell Holmes was some comfort, and, had the case occurred a few years later, when the flat assertion of the Sherman act that *all* agreements 'in restraint of trade' were unlawful had been modified by later legislation, the verdict might have been reversed.

The dissolution of the Northern Securities Company meant that its securities were redistributed to their original owners. The practical effect was small. 'Two certificates of stock are now issued instead of one,' Hill remarked; 'they are printed in different colours, and this is the main difference.' 'TR' was never really much of a trust-buster, but Morgan at least never forgave him for the prosecution of the Northern Securities Company. When Roosevelt left office and departed for safari in Africa, the great banker merely commented, 'I hope the first lion he meets does his duty.'

By the time the Northern Securities Company was dissolved, the dispute between Hill and Harriman was effectively over. Relations had not been easy in the three years since the crisis of 1901, and the break-up of the holding company caused some further conflicts, but a *modus vivendi* – not immune to all shocks – had been established between the railroads of the West. Harriman gradually sold his stock in the Great Northern and the Northern Pacific during 1905–06, when prices were high, and realized in the process a profit of about $50 million.

With these enormously enlarged resources, Harriman renewed his old ambition to create a truly transcontinental system which he would control from the Atlantic to the Pacific shore, something Hill never attempted – nor wished to. He gained a dominant interest in the Baltimore and Ohio when the Pennsylvania relinquished its stock in that famous old company, and together with the Illinois Central, the Baltimore and Ohio and its subsidiary lines gave him the great coast-to-coast system he desired. His empire attracted political attacks – from Roosevelt, who loathed him with all the loathing of the physically powerful, successful extravert for the physically slight, successful introvert, downwards. But an investigation by the ICC acquitted him of all charges (though without halting the criticism). Harriman went on to acquire more lines and to make the Union Pacific, which ten years earlier both Hill and Morgan had regarded as beyond human assistance, the most successful railroad in the country. His plans for expansion were ended in 1909 only by his death, worn out at the age of sixty-one. James J. Hill was not among the mourners at the funeral.

The day of the 'Railroad Barons' was passing. Most of the main routes had been completed in the 1880s, though improvement and expansion went on at a great pace. The Milwaukee, after long delay, finally built a third line to the Pacific North-West, at heavy cost, and Hill built his projected line from Spokane to Portland along the north bank of the Columbia River, which he had threatened Harriman with some years before at the time of the conflict over the Oregon Railway and Navigation Company. This, too was a very expensive project. Another line was built in sharp competition with Harriman (who died before the dispute was settled) in the Deschutes Canyon, to tap the traffic of central Oregon. Competition from the Canadian Pacific continued to be a source of annoyance, as in the days of van Horne, and Hill's tendency was to react over-aggressively. He built unprofitable branch lines to draw off the Canadian Pacific's traffic at various points, and even threatened a new transcontinental of his own between Winnipeg and Vancouver.

Jim Hill's magnificent Stone Arch Bridge at St Paul, built c. 1900 and still standing

215

The Union Depot, St Paul, one of the largest railroad terminals in the west when first built

But there were no new empires to build. Already, Henry Ford and others were engaged on the work which would ultimately restore the dominance of road over rail. Of greater immediate importance, however, was the changing political climate. In 1906 the Hepburn Act gave the ICC power to fix railroad rates, and in 1910 a Congress dominated by 'Progressives' passed the Mann-Elkins Act, which made it practically impossible to raise rates in any circumstances. Raising capital for railroad companies became more difficult. Hill recognized that the business had no future for men of his stamp, and advised his son Louis to get out of railroads before he was forty.

In the last decade of his life Hill was busier than ever. The first of his large Pacific steamships had been launched in 1902, but this eventually proved to be one of his less successful

ventures. He was still active in farming and conservation –
which in those days meant husbanding of natural resources
rather than preservation of the countryside. The railroad men
have sometimes been accused of luring people into areas where
agriculture could not be sustained successfully, though it
seems hardly fair to blame Hill and his like for the dustbowls of
the 1930s. Hill wrote a number of articles and a book,
Highways of Progress, in which agricultural affairs figured large.
He spent some time at his Quebec salmon-fishing lodge, some
on his yacht, and some with his devoted wife at a private resort
in the Carolinas. A bronze bust of him was unveiled at Seattle, a
doctorate was bestowed on him by Yale and, most satisfactory
to him perhaps, a new professorial chair in Railroad
Transportation was named after him at Harvard Business
School.

In his seventies, Hill gradually withdrew from active
railroad management. He resigned his chairmanship of the
Great Northern in 1912 (when he was seventy-four), but
promptly bought a couple of banks to keep himself occupied.
His old friends were disappearing: Morgan died in 1913, and
the following year Lord Strathcona (Donald Smith) died at
last in his English country house at the age of ninety-four. Hill
suffered from his teeth and from painful haemorrhoids. He
played an important part in arranging the American loan for
the British and the French in 1915, but he was not to be seen
again in his New York house on East 65th Street. The
following spring he became ill. Infected haemorrhoids led to
gangrene, and although he was operated on by the celebrated
Doctors Mayo, who travelled from their clinic at Rochester,
Minnesota, to attend him, the patient was too old and too
weak to recover from the operation. On May 29, 1916, the last
of the 'Railway Barons' died peacefully at his home in St Paul.

Acknowledgements

The following persons and organizations kindly supplied photographs used in this book. They are listed alphabetically.

Ann Ronan Picture Library, pp 22, 101, 103, 120
Mansell Collection, pp 39, 43, 51, 56, 63, 68, 84, 90, 115, 130, 174/175, 184/185
Mary Evans Picture Library, pp 16, 18, 27, 28, 29, 31, 37, 59, 70, 79, 110
Minnesota Historical Society, pp 162, 190/191, 192/193, 211, 215, 216
National Portrait Gallery, p 30
Peter Newark's Western Americana, pp 109, 112, 113, 116 (both), 122, 123, 128, 141, 180/181, 186/187, 197
Radio Times Hulton Picture Library, pp 45, 78, 89, 97, 134, 137, 143, 164, 200

Bibliography

Addressing an apology to inadvertently uncited authorities in his biography of James J. Hill, Albro Martin remarks, 'we all stand squarely on the shoulders of those who have gone before. I shall be greatly pleased if others use this book as confidently as I have used yours'. I have taken him at his word and hope that the other authors listed below, especially the biographers of the chief subjects of this book, will take a similarly generous view of the use I have made of them.

The following seven works provide a key to quotations specifically numbered in the text. Thereafter, authors are listed alphabetically.

1 Quoted by Philip S. Bagwell *The Transport Revolution from 1770* 1974
2 H. G. Lewin *The Railway Mania and Its Aftermath 1845–52* 1936
3 D. Morier Evans *Facts, Failures and Frauds* 1859
4 Arthur Helps *Life and Labours of Mr. Brassey* 1872
5 Thomas C. Cochran and William Miller *The Age of Enterprise* rev. ed. 1961
6 Quoted by Albro Martin *James J. Hill and the Opening of the Northwest* 1976

Charles F. and Henry Adams *Chapters of Erie* 1886
E. G. Barnes *The Rise of the Midland Railway 1844–74* 1966
C. A. and M. R. Beard *The Rise of American Civilization*, 2 v. 1927
Pierre Berton *The Impossible Railway* 1972 (i.e. the Canadian Pacific)
Thomas Brassey (Earl Brassey) *Work and Wages* rev. ed. 1916
Seymour Broadbridge *Studies in Railway Expansion and the Capital Market in England 1825–73* 1970
John Chamberlain *The Enterprising Americans* 1963
J. H. Clapham *An Economic History of Modern Britain* 2nd ed., v. 1 1930
Frederick A. Cleveland and F. W. Powell *Railroad Promotion and Capitalization* 1909
E. Cleveland-Stevens *English Railways, Their Development and Their Relation to the State* 1916
Terry Coleman *The Railway Navvies* 1965
A. W. Currie *The Grand Trunk Railway of Canada* 1957
Seymour Dunbar *History of Travel in America* 1915
Robert W. Fogel *Railroads and American Economic Growth* 1964
J. Francis *History of the English Railway* 2 v. 1851
Sir Walter Fraser *Disraeli and His Day* 1891
Robert H. Fuller *Jubilee Jim* 1928 (a 'biographical novel' of Fisk)
Heather Gilbert *Awakening Continent: the Life of Lord Mount Stephen* v. 1 1966

C. H. Grinling *History of the Great Northern Railway* 3rd ed. 1966
Julius Grodinsky *Jay Gould, His Business Career* 1957
M. Halstead and J. F. Beale *Life of Jay Gould* 1892
William H. Harbaugh *Power and Responsibility: the Life and Times of Theodore Roosevelt* 1961
G. R. Hawke *Railways and Economic Growth in England and Wales 1840–70* 1970
J. B. Hedges *Henry Villard and the Railways of the Northwest* 1930
Stewart H. Holbrook *The Story of American Railroads* 1948
Carl Hovey *The Life Story of J. P. Morgan* 1912
Willoughby Jones *James Fisk Jr* 1872
Matthew Josephson *The Robber Barons* 1934
D. Joy *Main Line Over Shap* 1967
George Kennan *E. H. Harriman, A Biography* 2 v. 1922
Richard S. Lambert *The Railway King* 1934 (i.e. Hudson)
Dionysus Lardner *Railway Economy* 1850
James McCague *Moguls and Iron Men* 1961
R. K. Middlemass *The Master Builders* 1963 (including Brassey)
John R. Moody *The Railroad Builders* 1919
H. S. Mott *The Story of Erie* 1900
O. S. Nock *The Caledonian Railway* 1962
Richard O'Connor *Gould's Millions* 1962
Richard C. Overton *Burlington Route* 1965
H. W. Parris *Government and Railways in 19th-Century Britain* 1965
F. C. Pierce *Fisk and the Fisk Family* 1872
Harold Pollins *British Railways: An Industrial History* 1971
E. A. Pratt *American Railways* 1903
History of Inland Transport and Communications in England 1912
Joseph G. Pyle *The Life of James J. Hill* 2 v. 1916
M. C. Reed (ed.) *Railways in the Victorian Economy* 1969
William Z. Ripley *Railroads: Finance and Organization* 1915
(ed.) *Railway Problem* 1916
Michael Robbins *The Railway Age* 1962
W. H. Russell *The War* 1855 (i.e. Crimea)
Jack Simmons *Railways of Britain* 2nd ed. 1968
Eugene V. Smalley *History of the Northern Pacific Railroad* 1883
John B. Snell *Mechanical Engineering: Railways* 1971
F. H. Spearman *The Strategy of Great Railroads* 1905
Herbert Spencer *Railway Morals and Railway Policy* 1855
John F. Stover *American Railroads* 1961
G. R. Taylor and I. D. Neu *The American Railroad Network 1861–90* 1956
W. M. Tomlinson *The North-Eastern Railway: Its Rise and Development* 1914
Charles Walker *Thomas Brassey, Railway Builder* 1969
Bouck White *The Book of Daniel Drew* 1910
Beckles Wilson *The Life of Lord Strathcona and Mount Royal* 2 v. 1915

Index

R stands for 'Railway(s)' or
'Railroad(s)'